The
National Plant
Collection

DIAL PRESS

First published 1993

ISBN 0 7110 2163 5

© John Kelly

The right of John Kelly to be identified as author of this work has been asserted by him in accordance with the Copyright, Designs and Patents Act 1988.

Published by Dial Press.
Dial Press is an imprint of Ian Allan Publishing, Addlestone, Surrey.

Designed by Richard Garratt Design, The Old Vicarage, Horton cum Studley, Oxford OX9 1BT.

Printed in Great Britain by Ian Allan Printing Ltd, Coombelands House, Addlestone, Surrey KT15 1HY

Page 1: **Azaleas at the Savill Garden, Windsor Great Park, home of several National Collections, including *Rhododendron* species and Glenn Dale azaleas.**

Page 3: ***Hydrangea* 'Mme F. Riverain' in the company of hemerocallis and *Lilium pardalinum*.**

Front cover illustration: ***Dahlia* 'Bishop of Llandaff' at Dyffryn. Its present great popularity is largely due to the work of the National Council for the Conservation of Plants and Gardens (NCCPG), under whose aegis it was rescued from obscurity.**

Back cover illustration: ***Gentiana asclepiadea*. The National Collection is held at Hoo House Nursery, near Tewkesbury, Gloucestershire.**

Glossary

Bigeneric
Of a hybrid between members of two different genera. In a trigeneric hybrid, three genera will have been involved, eg *Lyonarci*, hybrids in the orchid family involving species of *Cattleya*, *Laelia* and *Schomburgkia*.

Cultivar
Defined by the International Commission for the Nomenclature (qv) of Cultivated Plants as an assemblage of cultivated plants with any characters suitable for horticulture and which when reproduced (sexually or asexually) retains its distinguishing features.

This definition is inadequate, as it allows plants with only one distinguishing feature to qualify. This means that a cultivated plant, constant in its flower colour, whose seedlings varied widely in flower size, would qualify as a cultivar. Unfortunately, until changed it is the definition. Meanwhile, gardeners have to continue to use the term in their own way, which is virtually interchangeable with 'clone', otherwise it has no real meaning for them. It is, however, perfectly permissible within the Code of the Commission to use as an alternative the term 'variety'. Botanists never do this.

Genus
A group of closely related species (plural; genera).

Lumper
A botanist with a penchant for creating ever larger genera by robbing others (see Splitter). Usually a monographer (qv).

Monographer
A botanist who writes a book about one genus.

NCCPG
The National Council for the Conservation of Plants and Gardens; the organisation governing the National Collections.

Nomenclature
Names and systems of names.

Petiolarid
Refers to a group of Asiatic primulas that are quite difficult to grow.

Pharmacopaeia
A compendium of drug recipes.

Primary hybrid
A hybrid resulting from a cross between two species, rather than between a hybrid and a species or between two hybrids.

Species
An assemblage of individuals having characteristics in common that distinguish them from others within the genus (qv).

Splitter
A botanist with a predilection towards removing species from genera and creating new, usually ineptly named, genera. Likely to be a taxonomist (qv).

Systematic
Used in the special sense of referring to schemes of classification.

Taxonomist
One whose life's work is an attempt to order nature by placing living organisms into sharply defined categories. An optimist.

The National
Plant Collection

Contents

Preface

During the course of the research for this book, I have arrived at certain judgements and opinions that have inevitably surfaced during its writing. It is bound to be asked who this person is who blithely pronounces upon the National Council for the Conservation of Plants and Gardens and its National Collection Scheme. Accordingly, an account of what bona fides I may have is in order.

During the latter part of the 1970s, I was associated with the late Roy Elliott, then a member of Council of the Royal Horticultural Society, as the assistant editor of the *Quarterly Bulletin of the Alpine Garden Society*, of which he was probably the most distinguished editor. Sometime in late 1976 or early 1977 he discussed with me moves to convene a conference whose purpose would be to investigate the feasibility of organising the conservation of garden plants, as opposed to British wild plants. The conference was duly held in 1978 – by which time I had moved on – and two years later the National Council for the Conservation of Plants and Gardens (NCCPG) came into being. Thus, while not at first involved, I have been aware of it since it was a twinkle in the eye of its creators.

For most of the 1980s I was a member and then a committee member of the Dorset Group of the NCCPG. I was chairman of the sub-committee that planned and executed the NCCPG stand at Chelsea in 1984, and for some years held two National Collections on behalf of my employers of that time.

During those years I met many of the nation's best and most dedicated gardeners, both as a result of running a large garden that was open to the public and also in the course of co-presenting BBC Television's Gardeners' World programme from 1985-1989. Few people are given a better opportunity to obtain an overview of the state of ornamental horticulture in the British Isles.

The National Collections Scheme is about to come of age. It has passed through a rapid childhood and a risky adolescence, and has still not quite attained its majority. This book is written with the knowledge of the NCCPG, but in no way under its aegis. The views expressed and the observations made are my own; if the journalistic nose for a good story is in evidence, I make no apologies.

Tony Lowe, General Secretary, and Graham Pattison, Horticultural Advisor and National Collections co-ordinator of the NCCPG, have been pleasant and helpful and I am also greatly indebted to Pat and Philip Vlasto of Child Okeford, Dorset, for good information and for their unfailing good sense and kindness.

My thanks are due to Barbara Davies, of Stapeley Water Gardens Ltd, Nantwich, Cheshire, whose researches into Claude Monet and the Giverny water lilies were carried out over a long period. Also to Joe Sharman, Monksilver Nursery, Cottenham, Cambridge; Simon Goodenough, Ventnor Botanic Garden, Isle of Wight; Cormac Foley, Horticulturist, Irish National Parks Department; Emeritus Professor J.G. Hawkes ScD, The University of Birmingham; Peter Lewis, Padlock Croft, West Wratting, Cambridge; Edna Squires of the Devon NCCPG Group; Tom La Dell, Maidstone, Kent; Mike Hirst, Houghall College, Durham; Chris Skinner and Richard Ward, Leeds Castle; Jeremy Wood, Salisbury; Neil Campbell-Sharp, Marlborough; Charis Ward and Sarah Sage, Abbey Dore, Nr. Hereford; Paul Picton, Colwall, Malvern; Terence Read, Hales Hall, Loddon, Norfolk; Kenneth Adlam, Ottery St Mary, Devon; Anne Stevens, Ansty, Dorset, Jenny Burgess, Loddon, Norfolk; Ann and Roger Bowden, Sticklepath, Devon, and Ray Cobb, Nottingham.

Photographs were kindly supplied by Stapeley Water Gardens Ltd, Philip Vlasto, Alan Stevens, Ray Cobb, Simon Goodenough, Peter Lewis, Edna Squires, Mike Hirst, Richard Ward, Neil Campbell-Sharp, Terence Read and Bill Shaw.

All the other photographs are my own. I should like to thank everyone for letting me and my tripod clutter their gardens and also to let it be known that gardening people remain unfailing in their hospitality.

John Kelly
*Pound Hill, Crawley, Sussex, and
The Borlin, County Cork, Ireland*

Part 1

Conservation and the Gardener

Any fine morning a power saw can fell a tree that took a thousand years to grow.

EDWIN WAY TEALE

The ancient Chinese curse, 'May you live in interesting times', seems to have descended on late twentieth century mankind. We find ourselves threatened with the possible degradation of the systems of the planet to an extent that would leave us before very long with nowhere to live. The irony of the situation is that we know how to prevent, or at least alleviate the effects of our civilisation on the world, but those who govern persist in demonstrating mankind's most debilitating fault; burying the head in the sand.

Each government, taking the 'national interest' as paramount (naturally, as it is one's nationals who can throw one out of office), behaves in an individual way.

Each individual, believing that he or she can do nothing about it all anyway, behaves according to the act of faith that declares, 'It couldn't happen to me'.

On the other hand, it would be fatuous to expect everyone to spend all their time wringing their hands and making green noises. Perhaps the best attitude for the individual is to determine to obtain the best and truest information possible about 'the environment' and then, according to that information, to press, both singly and as a member of a group or groups, for the removal of governmental heads from the blinkering sand.

The garden violas are in danger of being reduced to just a few well known ones such as 'Jackanapes'. Photo Nicola Kelly.

A realistic view of oneself as an individual can lead to even more positive action. If the only contribution you can make to the health of the planet as a whole is as a mere molecule of the body politic, you can specialise.

Let me illustrate this with an analogy. I have a relative who is a psychologist. He does not deal primarily with the ways you and I think, but concentrates on one or two small areas of behaviour. He is a recognised authority on one group of nerve fibres in the brain, and also knows more than almost anyone about left-handedness. His contribution to the science of psychology is minutely concentrated, yet recognised as being of great value.

Applying the analogy to caring for the environment suggests that we can be proportionately even more specialised. My relative is one among some thousands of research psychologists in the world; you and I are just two among several billions of its inhabitants, each one of which bears an equal or fairly equal responsibility for the world he or she lives in. If not even each one among those billions, but just many, were to work in tightly specialised areas of conservation, governments would be outflanked and we should turn out to have done very well without them.

My general field of professional activity is horticulture. However, circumstance and opportunity have led me to adopt the full-time occupation of garden writer. My speciality, as far as conservation of the environment goes, lies in communicating to others how they can specialise. I do this in two distinct ways. One is to encourage gardeners to observe their own particular pieces of ground as personalised parts of the entire body of land occupied by gardens. What I try to propagate is the recognition of the area of horticultural land as being just as potentially damaging as that devoted to agriculture. Farmers are frequently slated for polluting their surroundings, but it is easy to target the big, bad owners of land perched on their tractors as they salt the broad acres with fertilisers – not so easy to make the individual gardener feel guilty as he forks in his handful of Growmore. The second way in which I nag about specialised environmental responsibility is by calling attention to the plight of plants and pleading for their conservation.

That should, you might suppose, be an easy task. We are all aware of the plight of the rain forests, many of us know full well that top-soil run-off in the Himalayas is leading to the destruction of species, and some of us are familiar with the probable losses due to further desertification. However, just a few are concerned with something distinctly specialised – the conservation of plants which, for one reason or another, are under threat of being lost from our gardens. My ultimate speciality is to encourage you to join them.

The question immediately arises – why bother? Who cares about a few chrysanthemums when for every bushel of grain harvested in North America, two bushels of top-soil disappear? Who gives a tuppeny damn about the egregious rose 'Blue Moon', when every day plant species that could form the foundation of an entire new pharmacopaeia are wiped from the face of the earth for ever? The answer is to ask yourself what you are good at in connection with the environment. If you are a whiz of an agronomist who can influence presidents, jump to it. If you are another Dr Pincus and qualified

Meconopsis wallichii, **now classified as a form of** *M. nepaulensis* **(see page 91).**
Photo J.M. Hirst.

to find jungle roots from which birth pills can be extracted – go ahead. If you are a gardener and think that Viola 'Irish Molly' is important because it is a beautiful living thing that should not be lost – do something about it. To think that such an effort is too small for your notice is arrogance. The sand is too full of other heads for there to be room for yours as well.

Late in 1992, part of Windsor Castle, home of Her Majesty Queen Elizabeth, burnt down. During the fire, the nation was abuzz with anxious speculation about the possible destruction of art treasures. For once, the concern had nothing to do with their value, except among those involved in insurance, but was all about the tragedy involved in the loss of precious artefacts that were part of mankind's heritage. In the final analysis, you cannot put a price on a Rembrandt or a Vermeer. You cannot recall Titian and El Greco and bid them to start again because fire, flood or bomb damage have destroyed their original works. When you look at Donatello's wooden 'Magdalen' in Florence, Leonardo's 'Madonna of the Rocks' in Paris, or a Rublev icon in St Petersburg, you are witnessing the heights of man's aesthetic achievement. To lose them is unthinkable.

It is not just in the recognised arts, however, that man has created a heritage of beauty that cannot be duplicated. To illustrate this we can consider a small, wild flower of Japan and China with nine rose-red petals, rather small for its glossy, leathery leaves, and growing on a shrub closely related to another whose young shoots were used to make a drink, known to the Chinese as ch'a.

Over many centuries the Chinese and Japanese bred the camellia until the nine petals were often a hundred or more and the flowers were as big as or even larger than their leaves. During the Muromachi period of Japanese history (1333-1568), camellias were among the most important garden flowers in that country of exquisite and exacting aesthetic standards. By the time the first camellias were imported to the West, the varieties concerned were already very old.

Among them was one that became known as *Camellia japonica* 'Alba Plena'. It was brought to England in 1792 by Captain Connor of the British East India Company in his ship, the *Carnatic*. It is a fully double flower of pure white with well over a hundred petals and is to this day the standard by which all double white camellias are judged. The clarity of its flowers and their delicate modelling are rendered unique by their setting among leaves that have a distinctive, graceful twist, seen in no other camellia. It grows slowly, and yet trees over 9m (30ft) high still exist in the open air in south-western England, exactly two hundred years later as I write.

If that seems a long time, one can reflect on the fact that 'Alba Plena' is recognisable in manuscripts from the Sung Dynasty in China; AD 960-1126. During that period, Edward the Martyr was murdered at Corfe Castle, Canute did his thing with the tide, Brian Boru defeated the Norse at Clontarf, and William the Conqueror changed the face of England for ever.

Even earlier, during the T'ang Dynasty (AD 618-907), the tree peony, or moutan, was the

***Helleborus* 'Violetta', an outstanding cultivar introduced by Elizabeth Strangman (see p 84).** Photo Neil Campbell-Sharp.

favoured flower. It was the subject of poetry, notably that of Li Po, who described a famous beauty of the day looking on as the many varieties of tree peony opened specially for her in the park of the Emperor Ming Huang. There was a positive industry of peony-growing centred on Loyang during the reign of the Emperor Wu (AD 684-705). The best of the new, double flowers of the season would be chosen from the Festival of Ten Thousand Flowers and sent, carefully wrapped, by relays of horsemen to the emperor, while the whole population of the town turned out to see the rest of the show. During the Sung Dynasty, the moutan rose to a pinnacle of popularity, with ten thousand different ones being ordered for the Emperor's summer palace. Those who looked after them had to be poets as well as horticulturalists, and gentlemen of the court were expected to be expert at the cultivation of the peony.

The Emperor Wu was an almost exact contemporary of Pepin II of Heristal, great-grandfather of Charlemagne. As Wu took his throne, far away in Wessex one Caedwalla formed a war band, ravaged Sussex, conquered the Isle of Wight with massacre, and set up his brother as ruler of Kent. Fifty years after Wu's death, there appears in British history a king of Mercia by the name of Offa. Humbling stuff, don't you think. Still, one should not forget that the eighth century produced Bede and the Lindisfarne Gospels.

Tree peony hybrids travelled from China to Japan, where they were further developed over the next thousand years, to appear in the West in the eighteenth century. Now that we behave a little better we are privileged to be able to have as garden plants peonies with such names as Renkaku (Flight of Cranes), Tama Sudare (Jewelled Screen) and Hana Kisoi (Floral Rivalry).

Where do you place such plants as these and the ancient camellias in the hierarchy of man's artistic achievements? There is an argument for putting them very high indeed, as they are, after all, living things. Furthermore, you cannot exactly reproduce given varieties of plants like camellias and tree peonies. People often judge new varieties of plants as being insufficiently different from existing ones to warrant introduction, but there is always some difference, no matter how slight. You can create double white

Novi-Belgii asters (Michaelmas daisies). Top left is 'Schoolgirl', right centre is 'Percy Thrower', and the lower one is 'Purple Dome'.
Photo John Kelly

camellias, but you will never get another 'Alba Plena'. What is more, you cannot awaken Sung Shang-Fu, the greatest of the Sung Dynasty peony cultivators, and say, 'Sorry to disturb you, Your Excellency, but we have lost our moutan hybrids and would like you to start again from scratch'.

Having now accepted that some plants can be validly regarded as works of art, then you must admit that artistic worth is a matter of degree, and that some plants may be greater works, while others are lesser. To return for a moment to the recognised arts, you would, I am sure, despair at the permanent loss of Michelangelo's 'David', the ceiling of the Sistine Chapel, or the 'Winged Victory of Samothrace'. But how would you feel about the 6th century frescoes in the Church of Santa Maria Maggiore in Rome? What about the strange animal pictures of the Douanier Rousseau? How would you feel if there were only one copy left of Dashiel Hammett's 'The Maltese Falcon'?

You might not consider 'The Maltese Falcon' a great work of art, and it is not, but it is recognised by writers of modern fiction as the seminal breakthrough that freed story-telling from literary convention. The Santa Maria Maggiore frescoes are nowhere near such significant art as the ceiling of the Sistine Chapel, but they survived a century that saw Rome under the heel of Goths, Langobards and Franks. Rousseau's creepy tigers peer from foliage that exists nowhere, yet you keep going back for another look at the work of the man who has been an inspiration for generations of untrained but talented, 'primitive' painters.

In the world of plants, there are man-made hybrids that occupy analogous niches. There are, for example, the laced pinks, bred by the textile workers of Paisley, Scotland, and the show auriculas, many of which were raised by Manchester cotton workers in frames in their back yards. There is no romance about them like the stories of seventh-century China, but I find it very difficult not to regard them as sublime works of art – don't you?

If I have made out a case for the conservation of the sorts of garden plants into which mankind's artistic sense has been poured, whether over many hundreds or just a few years, I must now do so for species. This is in some ways a far simpler task, as most people would agree that to see the extinction of a species of any kind, animal or plant, is to witness a tragedy. Every plant species is the product of aeons of evolution that can never be repeated. As the only reflective animal species, we are custodians of the earth and are, whether we like it or not, increasingly responsible for the world's living things the more we impinge on their environments.

There again, though, we must learn to specialise if we are to have an immediate, as opposed to a long-term, political effect. Whereas, as citizens, we may legitimately seek to pressure governments to prevent the destruction of mahoganies, that is as far as we can go. We cannot take mahogany seed, germinate it, and grow it in our little gardens up here in the European off-shore archipelago. However, it may well be that by growing certain petiolarid primulas and some species of *Pleione*, plants that are possible in these islands, we may be preserving them from the fate that awaits them as the Himalayan chain becomes progressively deforested and much of its top-soil is lost.

Jeremy Wood, custodian of the National Collection of Hellebores (see page 79), expresses with admirable succinctness another rationale for conserving species. 'It seemed to us', he says, 'that a collection consisting solely

Paeonia 'Rock's Variety' is very close to the original wild species from which countless varieties were raised for the delectation of Chinese Emperors.
Photo John Kelly.

of named cultivars, as advocated by one authority, would be meaningless in the absence of the species from which they were ultimately derived'. Take no notice for the moment of the word 'cultivar'; we will come to that later. What he means is, by and large, man-made hybrids or forms selected by man.

Suppose, however, that there is a genus of plants from which very few, if any, man-made selections or hybrids exist. Is there a rationale for conserving them, given that we can grow them in gardens, which seems to be the only way of doing the job? Take cyclamen, for example. Only one species, *C. persicum*, has given rise to plants much different from those you could find in the wild tomorrow, and conserving them is not a practical or desirable proposition, as each is an individual, raised from seed. Only one species, *Cyclamen libanoticum*, is, as far as I know, under much of an immediate threat. Others are thriving in the wild. *C. purpurascens*, for example, grows all over the place in the area of the eastern Mediterranean. I have even had to pitch my tent on a few plants of it, in flower at that, because there just wasn't any choice. *C. repandum* occurs all the way from the south of France to the coast of Croatia, via Corsica, Sardinia, Greece, Italy, Sicily, Crete and Rhodes. They do

not seem to be in dire need of conservation, especially as they are quite easy to grow in the garden.

On the other hand, other cyclamen species are decidedly to be preserved in gardens as far as possible. *C. libanoticum* is part of an entire flora that is weakening under environmental pressure. *C. rohlfsianum*, which comes from the green hills west of Benghazi, and is not a plentiful species, must be considered a candidate for watchful care as the boundaries of the desert change with climatic upheaval. The same may possibly apply to *C. africanum*, from Algeria.

Cyclamen africanum is closely related to *C. hederifolium*, the familiar autumn cyclamen we used to know as *C. neapolitanum*. In fact it is so close to it that hybrids are known between the two. If you are going to grow the African species in order to conserve it, is it not a good idea also to grow its close relative, so that the two may be compared and studied? To know plants is to care more about them; to know them they must be studied.

At this point, we have covered the reasons for making systematic collections of plants – as opposed, that is, to filling our gardens with only the plants we like best. It is a good thing to do because on the one hand it is a way of ensuring

Many *Camellia japonica* varieties were old long before being introduced to the West in the 18th century. 'Adolphe Audusson' was raised in France prior to 1877. Photo John Kelly.

Meconopsis grandis, one of the Himalayan blue poppies.

Photo. J.M. Hirst

Minature decorative dahlia 'David Howard' at Dyffryn.
Photo. John Kelly.

that the results of mankind's manipulation of the plant world for aesthetic purposes is preserved, and on the other it provides a means by which we may study plants in order the better to understand them.

But is this not the business of botanical institutions? Surely, the botanic gardens of universities and other academic institutions and the gardens and trial grounds of learned horticultural societies are the places for such collections?

True. And in practice most of them, if not all, hold and maintain collections for study, and some deliberately grow plants that are endangered in the wild. They are not, however, in the business of stocking plants that are of value as works of art or as testaments to mankind's desire to make flowers more beautiful. There

are notable exceptions, such as the Winterbourne Botanic Gardens of the University of Birmingham, where the formally arranged teaching beds demonstrate the history of the European rose – in which the search for beauty is paramount – but in general their purpose is, naturally, academic.

It is only very recently that the formation of collections in which beautiful, man-made or selected plants, along with their associated species, have been made on any sort of organised basis for the purposes of conservation and study. The idealism that led to this happening, and the way in which gardeners of all kinds became involved, from university botanic garden curators and nurserymen to ordinary people with full-time, non-horticultural jobs, is what this book is about.

Part 2

The National Collections: Beginnings

*Render therefore unto Caesar
the things which are Caesar's...*
                    MATTHEW 22:21

A glance at the account of Ray Cobb's National *Crocus* Collection (page 37) will be enough to tell you that the basic idea was nothing new when the inaugurating conference of 1978 outlined the requirement for an organisation such as the NCCPG. What had not gone before was an initiative positive enough to produce results.

The Royal Horticultural Society's Council convened the conference and invitations went out to nurserymen, curators of botanic gardens, representatives of specialist societies and many people distinguished in the fields of plants and gardening.

The conference, held under the chairmanship of Sir George Taylor, resulted in active moves towards forming an organisation, and in 1981 Duncan Donald was appointed Taxono-mist to the NCCPG, a position which was later to become General Secretary. Since 1983 the General Secretary has had an assistant, and in July 1984, further staffing was made possible by the Manpower Services Commission.

The years from 1980 to 1985 saw a nation-wide organisation set up with the following objectives:

To define the rarity status of horticultural plants so that those in danger of being lost to cultivation can be saved.

To establish definitive collections (National Collections) of specific genera to provide a source of propagating material and opportunities for research and education.

To list gardens containing important plantings or representing a particular style, so that the benefit of these to the community can be retained.

Part of the National Collection of hostas on display at Sticklepath, Devon.
Photo John Kelly.

Of these, the third has become for all real purposes a dead letter. It was naive in its conception, as it entirely ignored the simple facts of human nature. If a tract of land is under threat, that threat will always prevail save for the intervention of *force majeure*. The only forces capable of overcoming land hunger are power and money and they should preferably be combined. The NCCPG has virtually no power and even less money. To mobilise public opinion – in other words to call up reserves of power – is impossible without large amounts of money. Similar constraints apply to any clout to which an organisation may aspire when attempting to deal with local planning authorities.

By contrast, no power attaches to the possession of plants, unless they have commercial or nefarious applications, and then only because they are the means whereby power and money can be generated. Therefore little stood in the way of the NCCPG's attaining its other stated objectives.

However, inherent weaknesses in the NCCPG that were to become evident later on were established from the beginning. The headquar-

ters structure was set up before there was a proper constitution, and ever since there has been a sense of the bureaucratic tail wagging the horticultural dog. It may well be that some of the well-founded grievances evinced by local groups in many parts of the country have their roots in this initial error.

For it is felt by many that headquarters takes upon itself too many folds of the mantle of authority and assumes a stance that is unwarrantedly didactic. It is also widely observed that by far the greater part of a member's subscription is demanded as tribute (in its most precise sense) to headquarters. Furthermore, the greater part, if not all of the proceeds of plants sales, raffles and other profit-making events run by the local groups is sent to headquarters, in many cases leaving the groups short of money with which to fund further events. The somewhat curt, almost militaristic 'chain of command' does not sit well with responsible people pursuing a leisure interest, and the heavy central drain on locally raised money is resented – in some cases bitterly.

It is universally maintained that the name of the society was a great mistake. 'The National

Anemone x *hybrida*. There are three National Collections of Japanese anemones - in Hampshire, Kent and Essex respectively.
Photo John Kelly.

Council for the Conservation of Plants and Gardens' is a considerable mouthful and has now, with the lack of emphasis on threatened gardens, become partly irrelevant. Besides, how can the ordinary member be in fact a 'member' of a council on which he has no seat? In fact, the NCCPG's legislative body is called 'The Council', so you have the faintly ludicrous situation in which the Council has a Council. Another view into which you can find yourself forced is that The Council (i.e. the legislative body) is the organisation, in which case the Members of Council are the only members and everyone else merely associates.

It appears that a change of name is regarded as desirable by others than the mere 'membership'. It would be highly desirable from a public relations point of view. For example, the large marquee at the 1992 Hampton Court Flower Show, in which some superb stands illustrating the work of the National Collections had been staged, flaunted along its roof ridge a sign saying 'NCCPG'. It is highly unlikely that this would have meant a thing to the great majority of visitors to the show, many of whom might have been drawn into the society's orbit had the name been one that communicated a meaningful message.

If a name that does not drive people to universal use of its abbreviation can be coined, a considerable step will have been taken towards making the society more accessible. Furthermore, it would behove headquarters staff to define for themselves that 'public' to which they address their public relations. The reason for this assertion is that the membership constitutes the body of people most vital to the existence of the society and it is essential that they should not be alienated by a quasi-disciplinary approach. The most dangerous feeling widely held among the membership is that the central organisation is the society's least relevant element.

When all that has been said, however, it is essential that there should be a monitoring presence, otherwise the standards required of the National Collections could easily decline. It is one thing to start a collection in the first flush of enthusiasm, quite another to maintain rigorous standards over a number of years when you are using your spare time. The many nurserymen who are collection holders usually tend to

Meconopsis x *sheldonii.*
Photo J.M. Hirst.

Above: **Her Majesty the Queen visiting the NCCPG marquee at the Hampton Court Flower Show in 1992.**
Photo John Kelly.

Right: **Astrophytum ornatum, a member of a genus of cacti given to promiscuous hybridising in cultivation, and thus difficult to identify with the accuracy required of a National Collection.**
Photo John Kelly.

the plants and the records in their leisure time, as, contrary to many peoples' preconceptions, their work for the NCCPG would be loss-making if it were to be accounted for in the businesses. They benefit as much as anyone else from the occasional nudge from above. It is not so much the job done by HQ that annoys, as the manner in which it has sometimes been done.

On the other hand, this is a very young organisation. It has achieved a very great deal in a comparatively short time, and it would have been a miracle if it had not made mistakes. No member is more conscious than the HQ staff that a period of reassessment is now due. It is greatly to the society's credit that its name and methods of working are all seen as being capable of review, and this responsible approach is evidence of a strength that bodes well for its future. Plants may be tricky to deal with but people are much more so, and it is never easy to please all of them. Royal patronage, bestowed on the NCCPG after the Chelsea Flower Show in 1992, has provided great encouragement, and Her Majesty the Queen visited the marquee at Hampton Court in the same year.

Uncritically to praise the NCCPG at this stage of its development would be mere sycophancy. However, it would be misleading in the extreme to criticise without pointing out that all the evidence points to its imminent emergence as a thoroughly well run, balanced organisation whose essential discipline is generated by the sense of responsibility common to its members. There is both administrative and horticultural expertise at headquarters and a growing aura of happy fulfilment filtering both upwards from the membership and downwards from the permanent staff.

The engine rooms of the organisation are its local (county) groups. The first to be formed was in Dorset, whose newly fledged members drew up their own constitution. When this was shown to Duncan Donald, he liked it so much that it was adopted in its entirety as the national constitution.

Local groups co-ordinate the activities of individuals and organisations within their boundaries and themselves monitor National Collections. A collator is appointed to gather information from within the area concerning the availability of rare or endangered plants, whether in private or commercial hands. Most local groups issue news-sheets and hold monthly meetings, to most of which speakers are invited to talk on subjects relevant to NCCPG activities. This relevance is quite widely interpreted and in practice the groups put on excellent programmes of plant-oriented talks, shows and competitions. There is usually a plant sales table, where great rarities often appear, superbly cultivated, in the ubiquitous yoghurt pots so beloved of the better-off British gardeners, whose ideas of economy can be most endearing.

The Pink Sheet (see the account of the activities of the Monksilver Nusery, page 32) is a major achievement of the NCCPG. It is, in fact, a book, but started as a list of rare and endangered plants printed by chance on pink paper. Now just under 100 pages, it is a resource almost beyond price. That many plants are removed from it each year is perhaps the true measure of the NCCPG, against which criticism of its organisation and methods falls into proportion.

Another such measure is the dedication of the collection holders and the spirit in which the great majority of them conduct their collections and observe the obligations that attend them. A collection holder is obliged to allow those with a genuine interest in the particular genus access to the plants and records, and to provide propagating material whenever possible to those with a bona fide use for it. No collection holder is obliged to provide tea, offer a bed for the night, spend hours talking, show people round the rest of the garden, send them home groaning under the weight of gifts of plants, drop everything at a moment's notice to spend the whole day with them or lend them photographs. During the research for this book all these things have happened to me and I have to say that they are the normal experience of gardeners since the founding of the organisation. Gardeners are, with a few surly, untypical exceptions whose misanthropy is their loss anyway, generous, life-loving people with an infectious gaiety that is rarely found among other identifiable groups of people. One of the successes of the NCCPG, unforeseen by its founders, was that these admirable qualities have been reinforced by its growth and success.

There are still some notable gaps in the National Collection. The Cactus family, for example, is notably poorly represented. Admittedly, there are fewer cultivars among cactuses than in other groups of genera, but there are some, such as *Mammillaria elongata* 'Gold'.

Mammillaria is also a good example of a genus many of whose members are under threat in the wild. The popular *M. bombycina*, whose clumps of deceptively woolly-looking plant bodies are in every cactus-fancier's collection, is extremely well established in cultivation but is unknown in the wild; other species, more rare in cultivation, owe their existence to gardeners. Orchids are sparsely represented; there are no collections of the bigeneric and trigeneric, man-made, hybrids, and only a tiny handful of the 500 or so genera and 15,000 species of orchids are to be found in the National Collection. Other genera cry out for the security afforded by the collections scheme.

This is hardly the fault of the NCCPG. It cannot decree that certain plant groups shall be herded into National Collections. All it can do is on the one hand to accept into its portfolio those collections of suitable standard and relevance that are offered, and on the other to let

Mammillopsis senilis was once the only species in its genus but is now considered to be one of the many species of Mammillaria. At one stage it was in danger of being lost.

Photo John Kelly.

it be known that there are gaps that should be filled.

Collections are at the mercy of botanists, in particular taxonomists and monographers whose research leads them to publish authoritative views on where the lines of science should be drawn through the infinite gradations between plants. Nature does not recognise genera, species, subspecies and forma; they are inventions of man, and therefore imperfect. Because man's knowledge is always expanding, revisions of the system of plant naming are inevitable.

Recent technical advances, notably the study of chromosomes, have led to wholesale changes in plant classification. Almost at a stroke, entire genera have been dismantled and reduced to rumps of their former selves. Good examples of this are *Chrysanthemum*, which is now split up into *Dendranthema, Argyranthemum, Leucanthemum, Balsamita, Leucanthemopsis, Leucanthemella, Arctanthemum, Tanacetum, Nipponanthemum, Chrysanthemopsis* – and *Chrysanthemum*; and *Polygonum*, whose component parts turn out to be *Persicaria, Fallopia, Fagopyrum* and the rump of *Polygonum*. Who knows how many National Collections, so painfully gathered together, will end up being irrelevant because of such machinations? Many of the collections in Part 3 of this book (such as *Sisyrinchium*, described further on page 127) have been attenuated because of the transfer of species to other genera, some of which have been coined for the purpose. So far, the National Collection system appears to be rising above resentment and disappointment, both of which would be natural but serve no purpose whatsoever, and members are resignedly rewriting their labels and hoping that the botanists know what they are doing. There is always a temptation to think that 'lumpers' – those who tend to put more species into fewer genera – are usually monographers (fatter monographs), while 'splitters' – botanists who cut genera up into more genera – are taxonomists (more taxa). Perhaps that verges on the cynical, but it is very hard on horticulturists and gardeners when they have to be constantly on the alert for name changes. For holders of National Collections, of whom certain standards of taxonomic accuracy are demanded, botanic whims are a pest. Botanists would do well, too, to remember that the rest of the world is educated these days and knows cant when it sees it. While

Argyranthemum 'Jamaica Primrose'. *Chrysanthemum* has been broken up into several genera, of which *Argyranthemum* is one. It is the subject of two National Collections.
Photo John Kelly.

admittedly there were good grounds for reclassifying *Cornus canadensis*, it was a bit bombastic to coin for such a lowly plant the generic name *Chamaepericlymenum*.

National Collection holders must, too, be on the lookout for plants that are subject to Plant Breeders' Rights (PBR). This system, which is widely regarded as iniquitous, effectively allows the patenting of plant cultivars so that they may not be propagated for sale without the paying of a royalty to the raiser. *Potentilla* 'Red Ace' is such a plant. Should a collection holder propagate a plant and, not knowing it to be subject to PBR, put a couple of offspring on the plant sales table at his local NCCPG meeting, he is liable to legal action that might very well prove expensive. PBR has a place in areas such as those of rose and fruit breeding, where some degree of protection is essential, but when applied to shrubs, herbaceous perennials and alpines, it begins to appear incongruous.

I have made much throughout this book of the value of amateurs to horticulture in general and to the National Collections in particular. I am not alone in deeply resenting the patronising, arrogant statements otherwise eminent professional horticulturists and botanists have

made decrying the talents, skills and application of amateurs and proclaiming their unfitness to hold National Collections. Others join me (a professional) in finding it difficult to find ways sufficiently to emphasise the vast contributions amateurs have made. To name but a few, Reginald Farrer, E. A. Bowles, E. B. Anderson, Margery Fish, Lawrence Johnston, the Bolitho, Dorrien-Smith, Loder and Rothschild families and the present and immediate past Presidents of the Royal Horticultural Society, whose collective contribution has been massive, are or were all amateurs. Of the collections featured in Part 2, I would back all five of the true amateurs to equal or surpass any professional within the confines of the specialist fields they have studied, and against quite a few in terms of general horticultural ability.

Nevertheless, the part that professionals play is enormously important, and some of the colleges and other institutions contribute far more to the National Collections scheme than they could reasonably be called upon to. Among the most notable of those with multiple collections are the Somerset College of Agriculture and Horticulture, the Cambridge University Botanic Gardens, the Savill and Valley Gardens

Azaleas and hardy ferns are among several National Collections held at the Savill Garden, Windsor Great Park, for the Crown Commissioners, under the aegis of plantsman John Bond.
Photo John Kelly.

Sedum spectabile
'Brilliant'.

Photo John Kelly.

(The Crown Commissioners), The Royal Horticultural Society, Wisley, The National Trust, Brogdale Horticultural Trust (all the collections of fruit) and the Sir Harold Hillier Gardens and Arboretum (Hampshire County Council).

National Collections are held by a bank training college, a distillery, several borough councils, a public relations company, a major seed house, a National Grid power station and an Oxford college. Three collections are held, not in the 'Nation' at all, but in the Republic of Ireland. Of equal value are the collections held by some of the biggest landowners in Britain and those that fit into gardens such as a good

shot-putter might clear with a desultory practice throw.

The word 'heritage' has been badly mauled in recent years. It has been applied to post-war Odeon and the worst of Victorian Gothic; and non-pictures, unversed 'poetry' and motor cars doomed inevitably to rust have had 'heritage' tacked on to them as if such a label conferred worth like the touch of Cinderella's fairy godmother. The NCCPG – whatever it may come to be called – and its National Collection holders are not widely known for their contribution to the true heritage of man at his best, but they thoroughly deserve to be.

Ray and Barbara Davies:
Water Lilies

There can be few people who do not love water lilies. In cool climates, their sumptuous blooms have a tropical, exotic presence, while the furnace heat of the tropics seems cooled by the fresh greenness of their flat leaves on the water.

I remember places by their water lilies. A deep blue, long-stemmed tropical graces the small pool in a friend's garden in Florida, where sunbeds on the decking are never brought in, oranges tumble into the water, and cardinal birds flash red among the palm fronds. On the coast of East Africa, rectangular pools reflect the white, Swahili architecture and accentuate the colours of the upturned chalices. At Tintinhull, in Somerset, yellow and red hardy water lilies lie calmly under the sun of our northern summer and induce you to share their reverie.

Apart from some magnolias, water lilies are the largest flowers we can grow. Size of itself is no virtue, but their simplicity and grace make for elegant grandeur, rather than mere bigness.

Nevertheless, they do take up a lot of space, and to display them properly requires a great deal of water if you are contemplating any sort of a collection. Very few people have the resources, time or manpower to house a National Collection.

Ray Davies does. He is the Managing Director of Stapeley Water Gardens, near Nantwich, in Cheshire. Starting in 1965, as Davies Enterprises, Stapeley has grown to be the largest facility of its kind in the world. Its 53 acres include over 2 acres under cover and the 1.3-acre, heated pavilion known as 'The Palms Tropical Oasis'. This is a rain forest under glass with 9m (30ft) palm trees, parrots, piranha fish – and the world's biggest water lily, *Victoria amazonica*, whose immense, flat leaves are as much as 2m (6ft 6in) across.

Stapeley is a premier tourist attraction but is first and foremost a centre where lovers of water gardening can find everything they require, from hose clips and gate valves to bubble fountains, and from humble oxygenating plants

The Latour-Marliac nursery at Temple-sur-Lot in south-western France in the time of Bory Latour-Marliac.

All pictures in this chapter appear by courtesy of Stapeley Water Gardens Ltd.

Right: **Joseph Bory Latour-Marliac (1830-1911).**

Stewart as trout lakes. The work of excavating them was done by hand over a period of about sixteen years up to 1920. In 1935 the lakes were converted from trout fishing to function purely as ornament, and the great plantsman, Amos Perry, was retained to assist.

Perry's main enterprise was Perry's Hardy Plant Farm in Enfield, Middlesex, no distance from the famous garden of E. A. Bowles at Middleton House. Perry's always specialised in water plants, and the lakes at Burnby Hall were planted with hardy hybrid water lilies, some procured specially for the purpose by Perry, and Perry's Hardy Plant Farm entered into a contract for the maintenance of the lakes and plantings. By Stewart's death in 1962, at the age of 90, there were 57 different water lilies in mature stands.

Sadly, decline set in until, in 1976, there were only five varieties remaining in the two lakes – the Upper and Lower Waters. The dominant plant, 'Gladstoniana', almost entirely choked the surfaces of both lakes. At about this time the Perry dynasty was ending. Amos's son, Reg, retired, and Stapeley Water Gardens acquired their business. Ray Davies, on going through the records, found the agreement between Amos Perry and Major Stewart covering the maintenance of the Burnby Hall Water Gardens and contacted the charitable trust overseeing the gardens. The result was that Stapeley took

to about sixty different water lilies. It is an official display site for the National Collection, but for wide open water and water lilies at their best, Burnby Hall Gardens, at Pocklington, near York has no rival.

Their two and a half acres of lakes were created early in the century by Major P. M

Right: **Nymphaea 'Graziella'.**

Second right: **N. 'Amabilis'.**

Second left:
Nymphea 'James Brydon'.

Left: **N. 'Laydekeri Fulgens'**

on a programme of restoration. *Nymphaea* 'Gladstoniana' was gradually reduced to one large plant in the deepest part of the Upper Water and room made for the reintroduction of a wide variety of water lilies.

The retired head gardener, Raymond Slaughter, whose first job as a lad had been on the original digging of the lakes, was on hand to advise on which water lily varieties had been planted before Major Stewart's death, while Perry's records were also available to be consulted. Expert planting, in the available depths of water from 15cm (6in) to 1.2m (4ft), an intimate knowledge of the space each variety needed to spread, and a keen sense of colour and balance were all brought to bear in gradually establishing a truly magnificent display.

By 1988 there were no fewer than 53 varieties in the Upper and Lower Waters and it came to be highly regarded by the International Water Lily Society, the international registration body for *Nymphaea*. Within little more than a six-month period, the display at Burnby Hall was honoured by this group, whose members are to be found in 23 different countries, and was designated the National Collection by the NCCPG.

Teams from Stapeley Water Gardens, co-ordinated by Ray Davies, still look after the lakes and their plantings. There are now 88 varieties on display – a truly astonishing number.

The lakes constitute a unique habitat for the genus, much of the success of which depends on the high population of fish. Their original design as trout lakes makes them ideal for the Roach, Rudd, Crucian Carp, Mirror Carp, Tench, Golden Orfe, Shubunkins, Goldfish, and Bronze, Orange and Ghost Koi Carp that live in them and help to maintain the balance of plants and nutrients.

Beside the varieties grown at Burnby Hall, there are a further 100 hardy varieties grown at Stapeley for the collection and for sale. They range in size from pygmies, which need nothing deeper than a basin, to the most vigorous,

N. 'Laydekeri Rosea', a water lily whose name is often given to impostors.

which are capable of spreading to diameters of 9m (30ft) and grow in almost 2m (6ft) of water. Beyond the 180 hardy varieties in the collection, a further 100 new hardy hybrids are on trial for horticultural suitability. There are also 30 species and varieties of tropical water lilies.

The establishment of what is arguably the finest collection and display of water lilies in the world and its status as a jewel in the crown of the NCCPG could furnish an exciting enough story as it is, but events have moved along still further, bringing with them as intriguing a body of historical and horticultural information as it would be possible to imagine. In 1991, Stapeley Water Gardens acquired L'Etablissment Botanique Latour-Marliac SA in Temple-sur-Lot, deep in the south-west of France, not far from the rugby-playing towns of Agen and Montauban.

Joseph Bory Latour-Marliac (1830–1911) – he appears not to have used his first forename – was one of the greatest plant hybridisers in history, yet one of the most unsung and underrated. Before him there were no hybrid water lilies, but the vast majority of the hardy hybrids grown today orignated with him. In 1898 he received the Veitch Memorial Medal from the Royal Horticultural Society after winning prizes for his water lilies all over Europe and supplying them to grand estate gardens all over the world, including those of William Robinson and Claude Monet.

On his death, the nursery passed to his grandson, Jean Laydeker. Wars intervened, production inevitably declined, and further generations of the Laydeker family had little interest in the nursery. However, they preserved it in its original state out of respect and only decided to sell it in 1991. They searched for a buyer who would treat it as they had, and the International Water Lily Society suggested that Ray Davies might be interested. The result has been yet another restoration programme, with the original, geometrically arranged grow-

N. 'Marliacea Carnea'.

Left: **N. 'Laydekeri Fulgens'. Compare this photograph with the painting on page 25.**

Below: **N. 'Marliacea Albida'.**

N. 'Marliacea Chromatella'.

ing beds that once contained between one and one and a half million plants just as they were. The French equivalent of the NCCPG is working with Ray and Barbara Davies to establish a National Collection, including many varieties that had been thought lost but were found still existing at Latour-Marliac.

Among the most enthralling 'finds' the Davies made when taking over the old nursery was that there were boxes and boxes of Bory Latour-Marliac's records – in perfect condition. His sales records, library and the records of his hybridising have proved all the more fascinating as it had been thought that none existed and that he had taken his secrets to the grave, leaving no hint as to the origins of his hybrid water lilies.

Whereas the tropical species set seed easily and hybridise readily, the hardy ones are not grown from seed without some difficulty and are not kindly disposed to hybridise. Nowadays, Latour-Marliac's 'secrets' are recognised chiefly as an understanding of the necessity for such things as removing the anthers of the flowers on the first day they are open and dusting the stigmas with pollen from the other putative parent no later than the second day. He learned to cope with the way in which the poppy-like seed capsules ripen under water, releasing their seeds to the surface, where they are buoyed up by a gelatinous coating. There

are a great many of the small seeds and they float for barely a day. The hybridiser needs to be extremely vigilant and to be a neat hand with a net in order to scoop them up before they sink and are lost in the silt. There is no doubt, though, that flair, instinct, and that sure eye and exquisite judgement that is the hallmark of great plant raisers had to have played a very large part in his success.

We also learn from his records and writings that he was indeed no fool. He knew full well that his work could all too easily be cashed in by other, would-be hybridisers of water lilies. We now know that he decided never to release a fertile, first generation hybrid and only named and put into commerce sterile plants from subsequent generations, thus protecting himself from a proliferation of hybrids that would have obliterated all signs of his unique work.

Latour-Marliac's nursery was the source and Latour-Marliac the creator of the water lilies featured in the various series of paintings by Claude Monet. The first series, consisting of a dozen paintings of lilies at his home at Giverny, dated 1899 and 1900, was exhibited in 1900. The titles were repetitive. 'Le Bassin aux nympheas' was applied to nine of them, but the series was anything but dull. Nevertheless, the critics thought he might have done better to have varied his viewpoint, and he seems in later series to have taken the point to heart.

He enlarged his lily pond in 1901, obtaining permission from the local council to divert part of the River Epte at Giverny, and continued to paint and rework paintings of water lilies until 1924, when his eyesight was rapidly failing. He died on 5 December 1926, at the age of 86, having lived at Giverny since 1883 – precisely half his life.

Barbara Davies has found, among the records of the Latour-Marliac nursery, correspondence, delivery notes and invoices to Monet. They are from the Marliac nursery and signed 'B. Latour Marliac'. A series from 1894-1903 shows that not only water lilies but a wide range of other water plants, such as the marginals *Myriophyllum prosderpinacoides* (parrots feather), *Pontederia* (pickerel weed), *Sagittaria* (arrowhead), and *Caltha polypetala* (marsh marigold) were supplied.

It is certain that Monet's water lily paintings, of which there were more than 80, owe their existence to Latour-Marliac, as without him the plants depicted would not have been available. A series of large canvases was installed in the Musée de L'Orangerie, Paris, in the year after the painter's death, and his representations and impressions of water lilies are to be found in private and public collections in many parts of the world, including the Museum of Fine Arts in Boston and in particular the Musée Marmottan in Paris.

In 1887, the water lilies supplied to Monet were species. An article written in *The Garden* of December 1893, by William Robinson (prolific garden writer and owner of Gravetye Manor and its famous garden in Sussex) also found by the Davies in the Latour-Marliac library, contains an account of the development of the hybrids taken from correspondence between Robinson and Latour-Marliac. In it the nurseryman recounts how he was encouraged to attempt the hybridisation of water lilies by 'the wonderful results which attended the hybridisation of a host of other special subjects'. He started in earnest in 1879 and fairly soon obtained a hybrid with deep red flowers which, however, proved to be hopelessly barren, with neither seeds nor offsets. He turned in

N. 'Marliacea Rosea'. Compare this with *N.* 'Laydekeri Rosea' on page 25.

Burnby Hall Gardens.

water lily paintings, suggests that Monet had something of an inside track to the new water lilies, perhaps not so surprising for one who was already a good and valued customer and experienced with the genus.

Latour-Marliac's success at the Universal Exhibition gave him great encouragement and he set to work to make a cross that would produce plants with a red colour superior to any that existed in the species. He proved that *N. odorata rubra* was incapable of further improvement and then, after many trials and experiments, succeeded in attaining a hybrid whose flowers were of the same colour as the tropical *N. rubra*. The most precious quality of this plant was that it set seed.

He kept it strictly to himself and raised seedlings from it in a range of colours from soft pink to deepest red. They could not be propagated by offsets, but could themselves be used for hybridising with spreading kinds, and it was from these crosses that he obtained the series of remarkably hardy hybrids which include 'Laydekeri Fulgens', 'Laydekeri Rosea' and 'Laydekeri Liliacea' (his daughter married Maurice Laydeker in 1882); and several *Marliacea* varieties.

The seed-bearing red hybrid also raised the possiblity of crosses with yellow-flowered kinds and Latour-Marliac looked forward to effecting hybrids with 'singular shades of colouring, such as orange, vermilion, gold, etc.' By the time William Robinson's article appeared several had already been introduced.

That Bory Latour-Marliac had some true 'secrets' of hybridising is highly likely, although they were probably more to do with knowing which strains of species to use as parents rather than with technicalities. They were never revealed to anybody except his sons, grandsons and great-grandsons. The story of the very beginning of the hybridising programme as recounted by them and found among the records is interesting because of the part played by the great American horticulturist, C. M. Hovey. Hovey was a Bostonian seedsman and nurseryman and editor of *The Magazine of Horticulture* (also known as 'Hovey's Magazine'). He visited the famous horticulturist, M. Godefroy-Leboef in 1878 and told him that there was a water lily of a far more brilliant pink than any in Europe in a neighbour's garden in Boston. The neighbour had a monopoly and would never sell a plant. Godefroy-Leboef put 1000 francs at Hovey's disposal and, after a few

other directions, using only the most free flowering subjects as parents. Little by little – it was to take ten years – he succeeded with innumerable sowings in raising types that were 'in every way improved in the form and other characteristics of their flowers'.

'It was thus', says Latour-Marliac, 'that one of these new subjects (*N. alba*), fertilised with the pollen from the American species *N. flava*, produced *N. Marliacea* 'Chromatella', which has achieved such a high reputation'. Later, using the American *N. odorata rubra* and his choicest specimen of *N. alba* as seed parent, he went on to raise *Marliacea* 'Rosea', *Marliacea* 'Carnea' and the largest flowered of all, *Marliacea* 'Albida'.

In 1889 he took a collection to the Universal Exhibition in Paris where, he says, 'Their graceful elegance...was appreciated, and they came back radiant with the distinction of a first prize'. This date, set alongside the dating of the early months, received half a dozen plants. He generously divided his plants with Latour-Marliac.

These were particularly fine forms of *N. odorata rubra* and must be regarded as the foundation stock of most of the water lilies that set Latour-Marliac apart and which we grow to this day.

One of Latour-Marliac's 'secrets' was in the use of tropical water lilies as co-parents with hardy, northern species. Tropicals are very difficult to overwinter, and European growers usually either renew them every year or keep them in heat. An account, written in 1892 by a visitor to the nursery, tells us that it was favoured with a spring whose temperature was a constant 12°C, and that this was made to flow from October to April into the pond containing the tropical lilies, while the entire pond was glazed with cold frame lights. The water lilies, thus protected from both the winter air and cold water, were so well suited that they flowered throughout the winter months.

The records the Davies have acquired on behalf of Stapeley Water Gardens are important, not just historically or because they open a little-known window on to the affairs of Claude Monet. Many of the names of the hardy water lily hybrids have for long been suspect and there has been no weight of evidence with which their correctness could be ascertained.

The great wealth of material concerning the hybridisation programmes of Latour-Marliac will go a long way to help the work, in which Ray Davies has been engaged, in establishing which name belongs properly to which variety. Furthermore, the studies made by this great nineteenth century horticulturist are now at the disposal of others who might take up his lance and instigate further strides in the development of this queen of flowers.

It is not possible or desirable for all National Collections to aspire to the scale on which the water lily collection in England has been established. *Nymphaea* is a genus that needs to be displayed on a grand scale, but others, including many in this book, require no more than a small to average garden. However, the care, dedication, clear thinking and delightfully eager excitement with which this collection is managed can serve as an example to all holders and would-be holders of National Collections.

Such is the record of my labours among the nymphaeas. May my enthusiasm for the flora of the waters spread and induce many others to follow my example in endeavouring to extend and enlarge the domain of horticulture.

B. Latour-Marliac, 1893.

Burnby Upper Lake in June 1992.

The Monksilver Nursery

I n very recent years the name of the Monksilver Nursery has kept cropping up among plant-loving gardeners and has tended to be heard more and more over the coffee cups at group meetings of the NCCPG.

I must confess to having first heard of it and its proprietors, Joe Sharman and Alan Leslie, while compiling information for this book, in particular in correspondence with Chris Skinner at Leeds Castle. After that it was like buying a new car, when suddenly every other car on the road seems to be of the same model. The name of the nursery occurred with the frequency of the Big M on a US highway.

Joe's and Alan's catalogue is like no other. The nursery was only started in 1989 and yet the list consists of ninety pages packed with information and no pictures. Every one of those pages is a treasury of rarities, with new cultivars like *Lysimachia punctata* 'Alexander' (a vari-

egated form) rubbing shoulders with wild-collected items like *Malus* sp. CLD 417 (CLD is the collectors' code for the joint Kew, Edinburgh and RHS expedition to Chungtien, Lijang and Dali, in Yunnan, China, 1990).

This is no advertisement, much as it may read like one. The relevance of the Monksilver Nursery to the National Collections scheme is much greater than mere commerce. As you find so very often among nurserymen who are involved with the collections, mere monetary gain takes a back seat to the love of plants that brought them into what is not, on the whole, a lucrative profession.

To understand just what drives Joe Sharman and what his unique contribution to the National Collections is, it is necessary to picture a four-year-old child on his knees in his own garden of twenty feet square (6m x 6m). There he grew peas, red hot pokers, stocks, snapdrag-

Amaryllis bed at the RHS garden, Hyde Hall, Chelmsford, Essex, including several Pink Sheet cultivars.
Photo Joe Sharman.

ons, asters, sweet williams – and strawberries and gooseberries. It is hard to imagine the diminutive gardener, solemnly laying the foundations for his life at an age when most of us were yet to tire of play bricks, but he kept it up until he was eleven and his family moved house.

He took with him what he could and to this day grows the same irises and pokers. He avers that horticulture took second place from eleven to nineteen, and who would not expect an adolescent boy to find more joys in sports, records and the opposite sex. 'I only had', he says, 'a large vegetable plot and a smaller flower area. I started selling plants in a small way at sixteen, mainly herbs and wild flowers'. Second place indeed!

The educational options open to him were university or nothing, so he chose nothing for a year in the shape of working for the Post Office or plucking turkeys. Heaven knows what it says for career guidance in the late 1970s, but he was not even made aware of horticultural colleges until his 'nothing' year had passed. Within two weeks of realising that horticulture was actually taught, he had landed

a job on a pick-your-own fruit and vegetable farm for his pre-entry year and worked for two months at the internationally famous Hillier nursery near Winchester.

He so loved Hilliers that he returned there for his 'sandwich' year while at Writtle College in Essex and it was there that he became involved with rare plants. He read about every plant he saw or handled and knew where every plant was in the famous arboretum. At Hilliers Joe received abundant encouragement from experienced plantsmen and received many plants, as well as being helped to improve his knowledge and horticultural skills.

Joe started to write down everything about the rare plants and came across the Pink Sheet – the NCCPG's gazeteer of endangered garden plants – which at the time (1984) was published sporadically, a section at a time. It appeared, sadly, to be full of errors. He then undertook to put the Pink Sheet on his computer and to put in all the sources for the plants he had found and was finding in his travels to gardens and nurseries all over Britain and in the United States and continental Europe. Each entry was given a number for security and the very large,

Three great rarities in company: *Anchusa leptophylla* **ssp** *incana* **(Pink Sheet),** *Eryngium tripartitum* **'Variegatum' (available from Monksilver but nowhere else), and** *Astrantia major* **'Ruby Wedding' (the true plant; not a seedling).**
Photo Joe Sharman.

Part of a border at the Monksilver Nursery with *Centaurea pulcherrima* (pink flowers), a Pink Sheet plant from the Caucasus.

Photo Joe Sharman.

finished document was sent to the NCCPG. It was then, Joe says, that he thinks they got the idea that he was interested in the subject.

In late 1990, with the nursery under way, Joe suggested to the NCCPG that he and Alan should rewrite the Pink Sheet and that the printing work involved could be sponsored by the Cambridge Group of the NCCPG. The Plant Committee found this suggestion to fit in perfectly with their plans to overhaul the Pink Sheet, and Joe's and Alan's work was the ideal complement to that done by Sarah Smith over the previous years.

In effect, Joe and Alan edit the Pink Sheet on behalf of the Plant Committee, updating the nomenclature and removing the plants that become listed as available under the NCCPG's criteria. Wherever possible, they edit the descriptions of the plants and add descriptions where previously there were none – usually because nobody was sure what the plants looked like.

The Pink Sheet is now a ninety-page softcover book, beautifully published by the Cambridge Group. Its colour-illustrated cover and typeface announce a quality production, and the famous pink paper, as always, bears a fascinating account of the maybe, the might have been, and the wealth of plants that time has allowed to become lost or almost so.

However, the Pink Sheet is by no means the only contribution Joe and Alan make to the National Collections scheme. Joe himself holds the National Collections of *Galeobdolon*, *Lamium* and *Vinca*. The first two are deadnettles and the third consists of the periwinkles – not very glamorous genera but vital for anyone wanting rapid ground cover with interesting variations.

Galeobdolon is subsumed by some authorities into *Lamium*, with *G. luteum* becoming *Lamium galeobdolon*. Such things are the very staff of life to botanical taxonomists, confusing though they may be to gardeners. Between the

***Centuarea pulcherrima* with two other rare plants, *Hesperis steveniana* and *Salvia* 'Viola Klose'.**

Photo Joe Sharman.

two genera, or within the one, depending on your opinion, Joe has over thirty different dead-nettles for sale. By no stretch of the imagination can he be said to be fired by commercial ambition in spending time in propagating them. Among the periwinkles in the nursery catalogue, there is one, *Vinca minor* 'Sabinka', that no other nursery appears to offer. This happens by no means only among the genera of which Joe holds the National Collection; it is a frequent occurrence.

Joe and Alan currently have something like 140 of the plants that appear on the Pink Sheet. In the catalogue dated September, 1992, the Monksilver Nursery listed over sixty Pink Sheet plants. When you bear in mind that the Pink Sheet is a list of plants feared to have been lost to cultivation in Britain or at least no longer commercially available, this is an astonishing statistic.

The research, hard work and often sheer good luck involved in acquiring a Pink Sheet plant cannot be overestimated. That someone should have acquired sixty would exhaust the vocabulary of a Lady Bracknell. It is a superb achievement, rendered far more so by the fact that these are the ones which have been propagated and catalogued. What others await the light of Monksilver's day must be awaited with anticipation.

It should be made clear that Pink Sheet plants are not always dazzling to look at. They are on the whole good garden plants but, as Professor Joad used to say, it depends what you mean by good. Nevertheless, it is important not to be too much given to making judgements, as others may know of some very good reason for a plant's worth, such as the enrichment of the gene pool with long flowering, resistance to disease, or any one of many desirable characteristics that may be missing from the genus as it stands in gardens.

When Joe and Alan started the nursery in 1989 their aims were to make available everything that came their way in the way of quality material, especially rare and Pink Sheet plants. They were determined to resist any pressure to produce hundreds of the most popular items. It is hard in these days of the bottom line and government by accountants to resist such pressures, but the two men saw that it could only lead to yet another garden centre. This might have been potentially lucrative, but was an unattractive course when viewed in the light of the love of plants that they shared.

Curiously enough, during the recession they did very well, while those who had taken the road of which accountants would have approved found themselves much less comfortable. The nursery simply cannot obtain or produce enough of the rare plants to satisfy demand.

Every year Joe contacts National Collection holders. He sends them lists of everything he has in their genera and there then ensue fascinating exchanges of plant material. The benefit to the nursery's propagation stock and the collections is mutual.

Joe is beginning to be a legend. He is credited with having a photographic memory – which perhaps he has – and with being one of the most formidably dedicated plantsman most of us have seen. This is not to diminish the passion for plants of a Roy Lancaster or the extraordinary single-mindedness of a Jim Archibald. It is just that this kind of dynamo is something quite new.

Incarvillea delavayi variegata. **The species is widely available, but the variegated form is almost unknown.** Photo Joe Sharman.

Pink Sheet plants listed by the Monksilver Nursery in 1992.

The figures refer to the number of entries in *The Plant Finder*, 1992/93 edition. Plants with more than four or five entries are likely candidates for removal from the Pink Sheet as being no longer considered to be in danger.

 * indicates that the sole entry is the Monksilver Nursery.

Achillea grandiflora	8
Achillea millefolium 'Sammatriese'	0
Aesculus hippocastanum 'Pyramidalis'	1

Aster umbellatus, a Pink Sheet endangered plant from North America.
Photo Joe Sharman.

Allium cernuum 'Hidcote'	*	*Hemerocallis citrina*	3
Anchusa leptophylla ssp. *incana*	4	*Hemerocallis middendorffii*	5
Anoda cristata 'Opal Cup'	2	*Hesperis matronalis* 'Lilacina Plena'	7
Apios americana	2	*Hypericum elongatum*	1
Arundo pliniana	4	*Iris longipetala*	1
Aster umbellatus	5	*Leucanthemum vulgare* 'Maistern'	0
Boltonia asteroides var. *latisquama*	7	*Lilium candidum* 'Plenum'	*
Camassia quamash 'Orion'	2	*Melica uniflora* forma *albida*	2
Catananche caerulea 'Bicolor'	*	*Melica uniflora* 'Variegata'	8
Centaurea pulcherrima	3	*Nepeta mussinii* 'Superba'	2
Cichorium intybus 'Album'	4	*Nepeta nepetella*	3
Commelina tuberosa 'Alba'	8	*Nepeta nuda* ssp. *nuda*	0
Corydalis saxicola	1	*Origanum acutidens*	3
Decodon verticillatus	0	*Phalaris arundinacea* 'Feesey's Form'	7
Dendranthema 'Anne, Lady Brockett'	*	*Phlox paniculata* 'Orange'	0
Dendranthema 'Jessie Cooper'	2	*Phragmites australis* 'Variegatus'	4
Dendranthema 'Nancy Perry'	9	*Platystemon californicus*	0
Dendranthema 'Paul Boissier'	9	*Pulmonaria rubra* 'Albocorollata'	0
Dendranthema 'Tapestry Rose'	0	*Ranunculus acris* 'Stevenii'	0
Dendranthema 'Wedding Day'	3	*Rudbeckia subtomentosa*	3
Deschampsia caespitosa 'Vivipara'	0	*Saccharum ravennae*	*
Echinops ritro ssp. *ruthenicus*	0	*Scutellaria incana*	5
Euphorbia characias ssp. *wulfenii*		*Sedum caucasicum*	2
'Lambrook Yellow'	3	*Sedum yunnanense*	0
Euphorbia cyparissias 'Orange Man'	*	*Teucrium hircanicum*	3
Galega officinalis 'Duchess of Bedford'	0	*Thalictrum occidentale*	0
Gypsophila acutifolia	2	*Thalictrum tuberosum*	4
Gypsophila altissima	3	*Trollius altaicus*	0
Helianthemum 'Snowball'	*	*Uvularia grandiflora* 'Pallida'	4
Helianthus laetiflorus var. *rigidus*	4	*Valeriana alliariifolia*	1
Helictotrichon sempervirens var.		*Verbena stricta*	1
pendulum	2		

Ray Cobb: **Crocus**

Most National Collections present puzzles and problems, in some cases because identification is uncertain, in others because the plants are not easy to grow, and often because a comprehensive collection involves the tracking down of rarities. Bulbs, however, present a fresh set of difficulties because, unlike other kinds of plants, they can only be identified at all (save crudely as members of a certain genus and not always then) when they are in flower.

Crocuses are especially uniform. Perhaps, as a shepherd comes to know individual sheep which to other people seem identical, a crocus expert recognises species by differences in foliage and habit that would be impenetrable to anyone else. It is perhaps remiss of me not to have asked Ray Cobb whether it is so, but then I would not care to. He is the most modest of men and is resolute in denying his expertise.

That is, of course, the most usual sign of the true savant, and I am quite certain that Ray truly feels that he has much left to learn about crocuses. In fact, his knowledge of all kinds of plants is greatly to be respected, but of *Crocus* he is an acknowledged master.

Once more, we have a perfect illustration of the paucity of vision and understanding of

Crocus sieberi 'Bowles' White', which now appears to be regarded as synonymous with C. s. 'Albus'. Photo Ray Cobb.

those who insist that amateurs are not truly capable of the rigour needed in looking after a National Collection. Ray – now retired from his directorship of a large pharmaceutical manufacturer – is an amateur, but the quality of his botany and horticultural skills is a match for anyone. It seems curious that the abilities needed to master such disciplines are so universally judged by what we did between the ages of eighteen and twenty-one. 'What qualifications has he got?' is not a question that accepts an answer referring to fifty years of dedication, backed up by a mind trained in scientific method in another discipline. A reply quoting a diploma from some college or other is always taken as satisfactory, no matter what the reputation of the college or the record of the recipient since it was obtained.

Indeed, long before the NCCPG came into existence, this amateur conceived the idea of building up a comprehensive collection of crocus in order to make material available for serious students of the genus and with the aim of conserving, propagating and distributing species and cultivars that were in danger of being lost to cultivation. Where the professionals were who might have been capable of such a generous and well-founded concept is not recorded.

Ray's collection started in 1950 as a result of generous gifts of plants from Ronald Ginns of Desborough, Northamptonshire, who also provided inspiration. Thanks to him, Ray was introduced to some of the greatest horiculturists of the century – E.B. Anderson, Oliver Wyatt and that legendary figure among lovers of crocuses, E.A. Bowles, whose famous garden at Myddleton House, Enfield, he visited in 1954. Over the years many people have contributed plants, and Ray makes special mention of Dr J.R. Marr, who donated many species from his plant hunting expeditions.

Ray became interested in gardening in the same way that many amateurs unknowingly set their feet on the path that is to lead them to a lifetime of interest and enjoyment. His first house had a small garden and he started, like so many young people, growing vegetables to supplement the household budget. Herbaceous perennials were followed by alpines and then bulbs, and Ray eventually became a leading light in the Nottingham Rock Garden Club, which incorporates the Nottingham Group of the Alpine Garden Society. He became its president during the early 1970s, a position in

which I was to follow him for a short while, during which time I learned to admire Ray's diplomacy and to recognise my own deficiency in it.

Apart from *Crocus*, Ray has significant collections of *Galanthus*, *Fritillaria*, *Narcissus*, *Colchicum* and *Tulipa* and has been in his present house and garden since 1963.

He constantly recalls the generosity of the many people in Britain and abroad who have given him bulbs and seeds and says that much of the fun of collecting plants comes from tracking down potential sources. It is highly significant that a number of nurserymen have donated material. In a cynical age it is pleasant to be refreshed by hearing of such departures from worship of the bottom line.

The collection contains about 400 distinct species, sub-species and cultivars. The only species and sub-species not now included in the collection are *CC. boulosii*, *hartmannianus* and *biflorus* ssp *artvinensis*. The rarest in the collection are: *CC. pelistericus*, *autranii*, *moabiticus*, *hermoneus*, *almehensis* and *leitchlinii*, none of which, unsurprisingly, has

an entry in *The Plant Finder*. For some reason none is listed in the NCCPG's Pink Sheet of rare and endangered plants, either. Because of shortage of space, the named cultivars of C. *vernus* and C. *chrysanthus* are not included in the collection.

Above: **Part of the National Collection of Crocus.** Photo Ray Cobb.

Above: **Crocus abantensis**, **a Turkish species that can be obtained from one or two specialist nurseries.**
Photo Ray Cobb.

Right: **C. scardicus is native to the Sar Planina, a range of high mountains running north-west of Skopje in Macedonia to the Albanian border.**
Photo Ray Cobb.

At first, much of the collection was grown in special beds in the open garden, but it became impractical because of the necessity for keeping stocks 'clean'. Now, although the garden abounds in crocuses, they are mostly escapees from the previous system, and the collection is housed in cold frames, with less hardy species and those needing intensive care being grown in the greenhouse. Labelling is vital, especially with a genus that abounds in species that look much like one another when out of flower, and Ray has a system of accession numbers which appear along with the name of the plant and its source.

The collection is vulnerable to losses due to pests, diseases and what Ray is pleased to call 'inadvertent mismanagement'. It is typical of the man that he should cite this as a reason for the importance of having a number of independent collections as insurance against total losses. It is also an aspect of his modest nature that is now prompting him to encourage other collectors to establish National Collections that might leave him with more leisure. He has, after all, been retired for seven years and crocuses are extremely demanding and labour-intensive.

The entire collection, occupying over 500 pots, has to be repotted annually and this is becoming a burden. He has lost the services of two people who used to help with the work of maintaining the collection, and it is becoming increasingly difficult to carry out the necessary task of measuring the sizes of the corms of all the rare species each year. He intends to concentrate, if possible, on a number of horti-cultural and taxonomic problems in the genus and eventually to leave the conservation side to others.

We are fortunate in these islands to have a magnificent tradition of amateur gardening that is practised at the highest levels of skill and knowledge. Ray's many years of work with *Crocus* are in little danger of being wasted, and future generations of gardeners will be the beneficiaries of his dedication even when his collection is eventually in other hands. Paul Furse, plantsman and explorer, used to maintain that rare plants are safer in the hands of amateur growers than in large institutions. One need not necessarily entirely agree – but it is arguable that, in a world in which directors of such institutions are increasingly at the mercy of changing priorities caused by starvation of resources, he may at least have had a point.

Above: **A rare, striped form of the Iranian *Crocus almehensis*, a species not in general cultivation.**
Photo Ray Cobb.

Left: **C. weldenii sulphurea. Another species now regarded as part of *C. biflorus*. This form departs from the usual bluish tinge on the white flowers.**
Photo Ray Cobb.

Peter Lewis: **Campanula**

The late Noël Coward was famous for many things, but unforgettable among them was the rather inconsequential line, 'Very flat, Norfolk'. East Anglia is a somewhat indistinct geographical entity, but it can safely be said that Norfolk is not the only part of it that tends toward evenness of contour. The county of Cambridge, whose intellectual heart has enriched the world for many centuries, is as flat as a ballroom floor.

Well, almost. One has to take account of the Cambridgeshire 'Alps' – the Gog Magog Hills east of the city of Cambridge. Their heights are hardly dizzy – the chief peak is all of 120m, or 391ft to be more precise – but they do make a difference to the climate.

Susan and Peter Lewis live in West Wratting, amid a concentration of 'W' villages – West Wickham, Wickhambrook, Weston Colville, Withersfield, Woodditton, and the significantly named Westley Waterless, which is over towards Six Mile Bottom. If this sounds like a leg-pull, it certainly is not; such names are standard fare in a Britain capable of Toller Porcorum and Ryme Intrinsica. Waterless is not indicative of desert; merely of one of the lowest rainfall figures in Britain.

Up on these elevations it can be snowing when it is merely raining twelve miles away in Cambridge. When the city basks in sunshine, these putative escarpments, the would-be downs of Cambridgeshire, dress up in clouds like little girls trying on their mothers' dresses. Temperatures of -15°C, a frigid 5°F, sometimes occur and there are regular sequences of several nights at -6° and -8°C.

Those who think they know the area imagine Cambridgeshire to be all fen – black, boggy and bottomless. Some of it is, of course, and around Wisbech is one of the great centres for

Campanula ochroleuca, a Caucasian perennial growing to about 75cm.
Photo Peter Lewis.

Campanula 'Stansfieldii' is one of the best of the small hybrids, lasting in flower for weeks and only 15cm high. It is unaccountably rare in cultivation.
Photo Peter Lewis.

market gardening. The area in which West Wratting stands is anything but peaty, though, and the soil is Suffolk boulder clay. Peter Lewis describes it as like a sticky, intractable plasticine, 'Left behind by ancient glaciers to break the hearts and spades of succeeding generations in summer...or to stick relentlessly to any boot that dares approach it in winter'.

Why try to garden in such a place? Well, the county is a lovesome spot, truth to tell, and the soil at Padlock Croft, the Lewis home, has benefited from more than the usual degree of organic husbandry. It was a carter's garden, with stables to one side and a cowyard just down the road. Such an *embarras de richesses* redounded to the benefit of the plasticine, turning it into a highly fertile, relatively friable tilth. East Anglians have always been excellent managers of the soil; perhaps that is why it is such an outstanding part of the country for producing first-class gardeners, both amateur and professional.

The Lewises serve to confound the distinction between those who grow plants for love and those who do so for money. It is a distinction that seems to engage the concerns of the NCCPG, but it would be a great shame if it were ever to emerge that holding a National Collection demanded some evidence of 'professional' status. The complete absence of paper qualifications did not prevent Miss

Willmott, E.A. Bowles or Lawrence Johnston from becoming eminent horticulturalists, and it has not been unknown for diploma holders to have forgotten everything as soon as the gates of the botanic garden shut behind them. Susan and Peter Lewis are professionals – they own and run a nursery – but only as a direct result of their amateur interest in plants. They grow plants for love *and* money.

Their speciality is *Campanula* and its associated genera, *Symphyandra*, *Adenophora*, and *Platycodon* – the bellflowers. Peter tells a tale about gardens, serpents, and the woman giving

The very rare *C. troegerae*, growing at Padlock Croft.
Photo Peter Lewis.

'Gloaming', a variety of *C. latifolia.*
Photo Peter Lewis.

Below: C. **persicifolia 'Plena'.**
Photo Peter Lewis.

Below right: **The unusual, pink form of *C. lactiflora* - 'Loddon Anna' - has been a favourite since its introduction in 1952.**
Photo Peter Lewis.

unto her husband to eat... setting squarely on Susan's shoulders the responsibility for luring him from contented pursuit of ever-better roses, tomatoes and beans into the web of her enthusiasm for alpines. Whatever the motivation, the pair of them found themselves with very large numbers of alpine plants, among which were many, many bellflowers. The garden 'just growed', and somehow a nursery came along like another member of the family. Hearing of the National Collection scheme, then in its early days, they offered their seventy-odd species and varieties to the NCCPG, who delightedly accepted. That number is now around 250.

Their one-acre garden is plant-oriented rather than laid out primarily to a design. What governs it is the need to create environments suitable for plants from Mexico to the Arctic Circle; comparatively little is given the protection of glass, even in winter. Plants are grown in sunny and shaded borders, raised beds, screes, troughs and sinks, and in pots in the Mediterranean house, alpine house and, for the very few, a cool house.

Campanulas have a fascination that those who know them only from the border may not have experienced. It is probably better to become acquainted with the alpine species first, as they have a deceptive fragility that is absent in the taller species. Nevertheless, once you have a feeling for the understated, cool palette of the genus, and a keen sense of familiarity when you see the elegantly simple, bell-shaped flowers, your affection will spread to the more stately among them.

Most campanulas thrive on calcareous (limy) soils, although it is debatable whether more than one or perhaps two actually need lime.

There are in fact just a few lime-haters, including *C. piperi*, from the Olympic Mountains of Washington State, and the dainty *C. excisa* and tricky *C. cenisia* from the European Alps. What they all have in common, however, is an obstinate demand for drainage that is as near to perfect as possible. This is why raised beds are used a lot at Padlock Croft. The alpine campanulas have a great affinity for a rock called tufa, which is created when slow streams, highly charged with lime, become further slowed by accumulations of sticks, leaves and so on, which quickly become petrified, damming the stream even more effectively and leading to even more tufa formation. This was enough to cause an entire large lake to appear in the Wakan Corridor of Afghanistan between the 1920s and the early 1960s, and at some time in the past large deposits have been laid down in North Wales, where alpine enthusiasts, often after very long trips from home, can find it for sale. It is a very soft, white rock and extremely porous. Crumbling and cutting it is easy, and a compost consisting of one third of tufa crumbs and dust, one third leafmould and one third decent garden soil will provide the perfect medium for small campanulas. A fine flint grit, such as that used for feeding chicks, is a good subtitute for tufa for the lime-haters.

There are a great many small, alpine species. Some are only just in cultivation. Others, such as *Campanula samarkandensis* (from Tadjikistan, formerly part of the USSR) have been introduced so recently that we are only just getting to know what they look like. A few, such as *C. morettiana*, which grows on just a few remote ledges in the Dolomites, are so difficult that it would be unforgivable not to make every effort to keep them in cultivation. Then again, arguments for the inclusion of species in the collections – advanced elsewhere in this book – are as soundly based as ever. A student of campanulas, able at one fell swoop to overview the genus from *C. pilosa* from Alaska and the Aleutians to *C. rigidipila* from the heights of Ethiopia, could not fail to understand the breadth of its distribution. What he would perhaps marvel at, something which he would not learn in the herbarium, is that each is just about as bone hardy as the other.

It is also instructive to those who are interested in the genus to be able to see species that have become almost legendary and to realise that they can in fact be grown. The late Will Ingwersen, in his authoritative *Manual of*

Alpine Plants, writes what can only be described as a paragraph of wistful despair concerning *C. hawkinsiana*: '...this rare and beautful species from Greece never obtained a firm foothold in cultivation...it is always coveted, but is more often absent than present... unfortunately given to collapsing without warning'.

Hybrids and garden forms occur more readily among the larger campanulas than among the alpines, although one species, *C. cochlearifolia*, appears in several forms in gardens. It is a delightful plant, wandering with great restraint and hanging its tiny thimbles on stems like dark blue fuse wire. It is a mainstay of the summer rock garden, and it should be thought essential that the forms be kept true to name.

However, some 'professionals' are insufficiently amateur to stray from the bottom line, and it has to be said that careless labelling has allowed the varieties to become badly mixed

The biennial *C. moesiaca*, from the Caucasus, is occasionally available to gardeners.
Photo Peter Lewis.

Above: **The true**
Campanula
Raineri.

Below: C. **x** *wockei*
'Puck'.

Photos Peter Lewis.

as it has been distributed by the many hundreds, probably thousands, by the most reputable specialist nurserymen in the land over many years.

There are one or two hybrids of *C. cochlearifolia*, mostly with *C. carpatica*, an easy rock garden or front-of-border plant with upturned, wide open cups. Most notable of them is *C.* x *haylodgensis*, one of the purest light blues among flowers, and *C.* 'Elizabeth Oliver', another blue, which occurred in Mr Bull's garden in Nottingham in about 1970. I was at that time an alpine plant nurseryman, and he asked me to distribute it, naming it after his daughter. It is good to see that its future is secure.

The taller, border campanulas are altogether easier and not nearly as demanding as to soil and conditions. This amenability seems to increase in direct proportion to the height of the plant, and the larger rock garden campanulas are much easier than the small ones. The smallest of all are the most difficult.

At the lower end of the upper scale, as it were, are the many forms of *C. carpatica*, while the tallest campanula is probably *C. pyramidalis*,

up. *Campanula cochlearifolia* 'Miranda' has appeared in many false guises over the years, but its slatey grey-blue is unique. Peter and Susan seem to have the right plant, as well as the Pink Sheet item *C.c.* 'Miss Willmott', a pale blue, slightly silvered form from the Rhone Glacier in Switzerland. It is hard, incidentally, to understand the endangered status of this form,

the chimney bellflower. In all, there are well over eighty garden varieties of the larger campanulas in the Padlock Croft Nursery catalogue, and it is questionable whether there has previously been such a comprehensive collection in the history of gardening. Not the least of the accomplishments of the National Collections scheme is the pressure-cooker effect it has on creating pools of specialised knowledge. Admittedly it requires people of dedication who know how to retrieve, sort and store knowledge, but they must also have the child-like spirit of curiosity that leads them to try again and again with plants that any reasonable person would reject as impossible.

There have always been gardeners willing to become deeply involved with just one genus or group of plants and to emerge as authorities. E.A. Bowles and Ray Cobb with *Crocus*, John Blanchard with *Narcissus*, Collingwood Ingram with flowering cherries, and Clifford Crook with campanulas have all enjoyed or are enjoying lives full of other responsibilities and should be thought of as 'amateur'. Their interests all antedated the NCCPG, too, although Cobb (retired director of a large pharmaceutical company) and Blanchard (a solicitor) are current National Collection holders. Susan and Peter Lewis are among those whose expertise has been sharpened and tempered by their involvement with the scheme to an extent that would probably not have happened otherwise. They are in that same tradition of amateurism. It is not a word that should be used in a pejorative sense, but should be applied with honour to people whose love and knowledge of plants is independent of pieces of paper awarded in youth.

The Croatian *C. waldsteiniana*.
Photo Peter Lewis.

Ventnor Botanic Garden:
Pseudopanax

The story of the National Collection of *Pseudopanax* has all the elements of the best drama – recognition, dedication, pursuit through hardship, loss, and finally brave hope and determination.

Simon Goodenough bears a name fit for the hero of a dramatic tale. He is a Kew-trained professional horticulturalist and a plantsman of wide knowledge and understanding. He is in charge of the remarkable Ventnor Botanic Garden, which occupies a chine – a steep ravine running down to the sea – on the Isle of Wight. It is a classic location for mildness of climate but, unlike the gardens of Cornwall, western Scotland and Ireland, it does not have the heavy rainfall experienced in those regions. As a site for a garden in which plants from the temperate parts of the southern hemisphere may happily grow, it is ideal.

Pseudopanax is a genus of shrubs related to *Aralia*, *Fatsia*, and ultimately ivy. Its species and cultivars are grown primarily for their foliage, which is always striking, whether like large, spread hands, possessing three big leaflets, or with just one. Some species from New Zealand have a juvenile phase in which the leaves are completely different from the adult ones. The genus is native to New Zealand, Tasmania, New Caledonia, and Chile, and is predominantly from the southern hemisphere.

These are very uncommon plants in cultivation. They are not easy to raise from seed, unless it is very fresh, and need an almost frost-free climate. Botanically, they are not easy to understand, either, which is why there is disagreement among scientists just as to what constitutes a pseudopanax. Closely related genera such as *Panax*, *Nothopanax* and *Neopanax* have from time to time taken over some of the species.

I have grown two – *P. laetus*, which has leaves like a big, olive-green, smooth horse-chestnut, and *P. crassifolius*. The latter has seedling leaves only about 3cm (1.5in) long, diamond-shaped and coarsely toothed. The plant grows from the seedling stage as a bolt upright, slender pole with leaves towards the top that are like serrated knives up to 90cm (3ft) long but only 3cm (1.5in) or so wide. They are leathery, reflexed somewhat downwards and the teeth are sharply pointed. When the tree – for it is one, rather than a shrub – starts to branch, the leaves change again. Some have three leaflets, while others have only one, but all are only half as long and instead of being downwardly deflected are upright, rather as if an umbrella had been blown inside out and then shrunk. Finally, there is a fourth stage, when the leaves are mostly toothless, are not divided into leaflets, and are about 15cm (6in)

The path down to Cathedral Caves in *Pseudopanax* habitat, New Zealand.
Photo Simon Goodenough.

long. Flowering begins when the trees start branching.

That is the extent of my knowledge of and experience with the genus *Pseudopanax*, but I can vouch for its fascination, which took hold of Simon when, in 1976, he visited Castlewellan, the noted garden and arboretum in Northern Ireland. There, the finest specimen of *P. laetus* in the British Isles is to be found. Simon was astounded by the appearance of the plant, and his imminent induction at Kew gave him the opportunity to study the genus and its distribution.

Towards the end of his time at Kew, Simon was in charge of the Temperate and Arboretum nursery and it was there that he began to grow a wider range of the species than had hitherto been achieved. He learned to understand the low viability of the seed, but it took some time and experimentation.

When he took up his position at Ventnor in 1985, there were maturing specimens of *P. chathamicus, P. crassifolius, P. ferox* and *P. laetus*. This was the largest gathering of species that Simon had hitherto seen out of doors as large specimens anywhere in the United Kingdom. This, the fact that they seemed to be doing so well, and his previous special interest in the genus, convinced him that Ventnor should take on the National Collection of *Pseudopanax*. He contacted the NCCPG, who lost little time in

sending him all the information they had on the genus, but it was indeed very little.

Undaunted, Simon began to contact friends in New Zealand and slowly seed began to arrive, along with a great many letters. His understanding of the genus and its distribution grew with the stack of correspondence.

He discovered that there are probably fourteen species endemic to New Zealand and something like twenty species all told. Only half the New Zealand species were represented in living collections and were only to be found in the wild. Today, the situation has improved, but nobody has as yet obtained material of all the known New Zealand species.

However, in 1987 Simon and his wife set off for New Zealand. This in itself was no mean undertaking, but their dedication and love of plants was the spur that led them to commit themselves to a great deal of backpacking in difficult terrain. Bear in mind that these are not the most easy plants to recognise and they were not able to go along to see them in a botanic garden beforehand. Furthermore, the New Zealand flora is lush and diverse, and spotting a genus of shrubs that changes the shape of its leaves and has flowers that are insignificant was like trying to identify a particular commuter on London Bridge at nine o'clock in the morning.

They received valuable help with locations from the scientific and forestry services but even so the task of accurately identifying species and finding them in fruit so that seed could be gathered was very difficult. *Pseudopanax* species have limited distribution and once the right areas were found identification was made even more tricky by the fact that the more

Left: **New Zealand: west coast rain-forest, where *Pseudopanax* species may be found.**
Photo Simon Goodenough.

Below: **West coast rain forest: The strange foliage of a pseudopanax above that of a tree fern.**
Photo Simon Goodenough.

**Part of the New
Zealand collection
at Ventnor
Botanic Garden.**
Photo Simon
Goodenough.

common species hybridise with maddening ease.

The Goodenoughs overcame all kinds of further problems and setbacks in establishing the National Collection, not the least of which was the discovery that field mice adore *Pseudopanax* seed. The great storm of October 1987 destroyed or badly damaged many of their mature plants at Ventnor, but they pressed on, raising new plants from seed, their optimism undiminished.

By 1990 they had a good selection of the genus, completely unrivalled in the UK, including most of the named cultivars introduced to the country by Messrs Duncan & Davies, the famous New Zealand nursery who have agents in Britain. You might think from my description that *Pseudopanax* are a little recherché as garden plants, but they are ideally suited when treated as exotic, extremely unusual foliage plants for the conservatory. They are far hardier than many *Ficus* and *Schefflera* – other genera with wide, deeply lobed leaves – and are extremely tolerant of low light levels.

Simon sums up his view of the collection thus: 'We as the collection holders are under no illusions as to the stature of the genus in terms of garden merit but notwithstanding this the development of a National Collection of such plants has at its heart the main aims of the collection scheme: to conserve these plants, to have the best and most representative collection of the genus for study at all levels and for all reasons, scientific, historic and artistic, and of course to experience the pure joy of growing plants to make them more widely available to gardeners'.

By 1991 the Ventnor collection of *Pseudopanax* had grown to include eleven species from New Zealand, one from Chile, one from Tasmania, eight cultivars from New Zealand, and several un-named hybrids. In the August of 1992 they were only two species short of having an entire collection of the genus, excluding one from China, which Simon considers to belong to the genus *Panax*.

In September, 1992, an entire representative collection of the *Pseudopanax* at Ventnor was stolen, leaving it without the Tasmanian and Chilean species. It meant the loss of three further species and two botanical varieties as well as two of the named cultivars from New Zealand. The autumn propagation programme that would have preserved these and other species and allowed them to be made available to other gardens was about to start; as a result of this cynical and callous theft, it could not take place.

Simon Goodenough estimates that the work of the collection has been put back by six years.

He remains determined to strive, in his own words, for the most representative collection he can, with a view to making the plants more widely known and available.

It is my fervent hope that the thief or thieves read this. They are obviously knowledgeable and knew exactly what to steal, but I hope that they will have great difficulty in selling or showing off their rare *Pseudopanax*. Someone reading this book is certain to come across them. They should hide the plants well, because otherwise they will certainly be found out. Field mice may in their innocence take the seed, but only those with the morals and standards of rats steal the product of a decent couple's dedication.

After the theft the National Collection of *Pseudopanax* consisted of the following:-

P. arboreus
P. discolor
P. chathamicus
P. crassifolius
P. ferox
P. gillesii
P. laetus
P. macintyrei
P. simplex
P. lessonii
P. lessonii – 'Gold Splash'

Ventnor Botanic Garden; a collection of phormiums.
Photo Simon Goodenough.

P. lessonii – 'Adiantifolius'
P. lessonii – 'Cyril Watson'
P. lessonii – 'Linearifolius'
P. lessonii – 'Trident'

Ventnor Botanic Garden; the New Zealand lawn viewed from the hydrangea dell.
Photo Simon Goodenough.

The University of Birmingham: The History of the European Rose

'Jacques Cartier', a Portland Rose of 1868 (Moreau-Robert).

Photo John Kelly.

There is currently an insidious fashion for large gardens in which are gathered unusual species and varieties of plants to be called (always with capital letters, of course), Botanic Gardens. They are nothing of the sort.

Just as you cannot dub yourself a knight or take the title of countess without certain essential procedures or qualifications of birth, you cannot just decide that your garden is a Botanic Garden because you think it is botanically interesting. Well, you can, but the world will think your senses have taken leave of you.

When I was a boy, I lived in a Welsh seaside town in which, I am sure, the nuances of the English language remained impenetrable to the local burghers. Hearing, for example, that supermarkets were the coming thing, they sold sites for stalls in an arcade that led to the promenade and had erected above its entrance a sign that proclaimed the 'Super Market'. Long before my time there had been a Winter Garden that was entirely open to the elements and closed from October to May. It was later renamed the Summer Gardens, but still went bust. Beyond the railway was another public garden. It had bowling greens, tennis courts, and little narrow beds round the edges with lobelia and alyssum planted in depressingly

hackneyed succession. There was, I remember, a wider affair altogether, in which pride of place went to an elderly clump of what we called pompous grass. This garden – it was a recreation ground, really – was grandiloquently called The Botanic Gardens. To me and my pals is was the tanny gardens, and I expect it still is.

Strictly speaking, a botanic garden is schematic. What that means is that it is laid out so that the plantings are grouped according to a plan that accords with academic study. Thus, you may find a series of beds, often called Order beds, each of which is devoted to one plant family – Graminae, Cruciferae, and so on. Alternatively the beds may be arranged so as to illustrate some other aspect of botany, as in the botanic garden of Clusius, which is maintained as part of the Botanic Garden of the University of Leiden, Holland. There his original, early seventeenth-century schematic beds, in which he set out the results of tulip breeding, are preserved. The Chelsea Physic Garden, in London, is a small botanic garden originally devoted to the study of medicinal plants. In part, it still consists of schematic teaching beds, called in Latin, *pulvulli*. Today, botanic gardens do not have to be as formal, and you will find the Botanic Garden at Cambridge University, for instance, to be one of the most aesthetically pleasing gardens you could wish for, with a beautiful small lake, a magnificent rock garden, and lovely walks among the trees. Nevertheless, its layout is entirely consistent with the academic study of plants. The Ventnor Botanic Garden, on the Isle of Wight, is entirely ornamental, but is at the same time planted so as to facilitate the study of tender plants from the southern hemisphere. Often, though, the most modern botanic gardens happily resort to teaching beds when that is the best way of encouraging study.

A part of the Botanic Gardens of the University of Birmingham is laid out with 32 rectangular beds in an austere, geometrical pattern, broken only by the circular shape of the central fountain. There is nothing grim about this mathematical rigidity, however, as the beds are a celebration of roses; a wonderfully colourful parade of the history of the rose as a garden plant in Europe, set out certainly for study (and what a fascinating study it is) but also for anyone with an eye for beauty to enjoy immensely.

These are *pulvulli*, and a very fine and classic example of them, too. However, they are not

Damask Rose 'Rose de Resht'. Photo John Kelly.

there just for the students, but also for anyone with a real interest in roses. It is a National Collection, and can be viewed by arrangement with the curator, who looks after it on behalf of the School of Continuing Studies. Remarkably, the collection was formed by one man, the Emeritus Professor J.G. Hawkes.

When discussing garden roses, the general conventions used in writing plant names go

The Alba Rose, 'Koenigin von Dänemarck', was raised by Booth in 1826. Photo John Kelly.

Gallica rose 'Belle de Crécy' has been in gardens since before 1848.
Photo John Kelly.

'Mme Pierre Oger', a classic Bourbon Rose (Oger, 1878).
Photo John Kelly.

some distance out of the window. For example, the Autumn Damask rose is referred to as *Rosa bifera,* as if it were a species. In fact it is a hybrid between two species; *Rosa gallica* and *Rosa moschata.* The White Rose of York, *Rosa alba,* is a hybrid between *R. damascena* and *R. canina,* but *R. damascena* itself is a hybrid, a marriage between *R. gallica* and *R. phoenicia.*

Rosa gallica, also known as *Rosa rubra,* is probably the oldest garden rose of all, and is certainly the foundation species of the European roses. It and three other species, *R. moschata* (the musk rose), *R. phoenicia,* and *R. canina* (our native dog rose), gave rise to all the ancient European garden roses. It was not until the latter part of the 18th century that roses from the Far East were introduced that revolutionised the rose and set its feet on the road to becoming the modern flower we know today.

Rosa gallica is thought to have been cultivated in the Persian Empire as long ago as the time of the Median Fire Worshippers in the 12th century BC, who grew it for use in their ceremonies. Later, the ancient Greeks grew it, and according to Pliny, the Romans knew it as a vivid red flower with twelve petals or less. The Provins rose, which retains its perfume when dried and was the basis of an entire industry in France for 600 years, was a variety of *R. gallica,* and it produced a bud sport with striped petals, which we know as 'Rosa Mundi'.

Rosa gallica is represented in the National Collection by many hybrids, mostly dating from the nineteenth century, but also by 'Officinalis', which was the Apothecary's Rose of Provins, and from which 'Rosa Mundi' – also present – sprang. It is a fine garden shrub, the flowers are a good crimson, and it is the best point of all from which to start a trip through the history of everyone's favourite garden flower.

After the beds containing the gallicas come three devoted to the Damasks. There are two groups of Damasks, the Summer Damasks (*R. gallica* x *R. phoenicia*), known as *R. damascena,* and the Autumn Damasks, which are *R. bifera* (*R. gallica* x *R. moschata*).

The Summer Damasks include some of the most exquisite of the 19th century roses, such as the wonderfully scented 'Madame Hardy', whose spotlessly white blooms are packed with petals arranged in 'quartered' whorls. Among them, too, are the rose called 'Kazanlik', which is grown in Bulgaria for the production of attar of roses, and the York and Lancaster rose, *R. damascena versicolor*, from which are supposed to have been plucked the favours – red and white – before the commencement of the Wars of the Roses between the Houses of Lancaster and York. You can go to Birmingham today and see this plant growing as it did then, as well as the gallica and the alba that became established as the badges of the factions.

'Quatre Saisons' is a rather optimistically named Damask rose. It certainly does not flower all year round, but does so from June to October, and was thus quite extraordinary in that long era before repeat-flowering roses became the standard. It occurs from time to time as a reversion on 'Quatre Saisons Blanc Mousseux', the 'Perpetual White Moss', and is thought to be the original Autumn Damask.

After the Damasks come the Albas – and you are still only up to beds nine and ten. The Albas descend from crosses between *R. damascena* and *R. canina*, and the latter is present to remind us of this. *R. alba semi-plena* is one of the oldest, with a beautiful habit of growth and semi-double, white flowers with golden stamens. It is another of the roses from which attar of roses is distilled at Kazanlik. 'Maiden's Blush' dates back to 1738, and is, like all Albas, ideal for growing in shade, where few roses will flower well. Among the nineteenth-century Albas grown in the collection is 'Queen of Denmark', quite one of the most beautiful roses of all time.

The *Centifolias* are the Cabbage roses, flowers so packed with petals that you wonder how there could be room for them. Those used to the modern roses with their high-crowned blooms might find it difficult to imagine, but if you, in your mind's eye, take a very sharp razor and cut a just-opened modern bloom across about one third of the way down from the tip, the result might be something similar. One of the *Centifolias* in the collection, called – somewhat dubiously, I think – 'Old Cabbage', is said to date from 1583.

In the *Centifolias* we begin to see the muta-

tions of the calyx that hint at the Moss roses. *R. centifolia cristata* (and I remind you again that these names are conventional, rather than scientific), has its calyces enlarged and furnished with strange crests. In the Moss roses the calyces are covered with what appears for all the world like green moss, and the first of these to be seen was *R. centifolia muscosa*, which made its debut in 1727 and is now known as 'Old Pink Moss'. The collection boasts fourteen different Moss roses, the youngest of which is 'Blanche Moreau' (1880), a beautiful rose in which the pure white flowers contrast tellingly with the moss, which in its case is brown.

Beds 15 to 18 and Bed 20 depict what some see as a tragic time in the history of the European rose, and others the most significant and welcome development imaginable. The introduction of the China roses (*Rosa chinensis*) as the 18th century turned into the 19th, gave rise to the Bourbon roses, which became widely

'Buff Beauty' is a Hybrid Musk rose of unknown parentage, introduced in 1939. Photo John Kelly.

popular because of the repeat-flowering habit (remontance) they inherited from them. Rather like the provenance of thoroughbred horses, all of which go back to five main sires, Bourbons and their descendants trace their ancestry back to hybrids of the old roses with 'Slater's Crimson China', 'Parson's Pink China', 'Hume's Blush Tea-Scented China', and 'Parks's Yellow Tea-Scented China'. The tea scent came from the Chinese species, *R. odorata* (syn *R. gigantea*).

These roses, together with *R. foetida bicolor* ('Austrian Copper') virtually initiated yellow as a colour in garden roses, although it was many years before the latter's influence came truly to be felt. Its double form, called 'Persian Yellow', was of brilliant colouring and was crossed with a Hybrid Perpetual in 1888. From the resulting seedlings Pernet produced in 1900 the Hybrid Tea 'Soleil d'Or', from which all our modern bright yellow and orange roses descend. Among the old garden roses, the only yellow prior to the introduction of 'Persian Yellow' was *Rosa hemisphaerica*, the Cabbage-rose-like Sulphur rose, which was introduced before 1625. It needs a warm climate to make it flower properly and Redouté was able to find it enjoying itself enough to be the subject of a sumptuous painting.

Progress – if that is what it was – was rapid after the introduction of the China roses. The earlier Bourbons, such as 'Bourbon Queen', had enough of the old rose appearance and characteristics to be assets to gardens of old European roses, as they flowered all summer long and their palette was in keeping. Later roses such as 'Mme Isaac Pereire' stood out from the company of another era rather like a Barbara Cartland figure at a Brontë tea party.

The Bourbons were followed by the Hybrid Perpetuals – annually pruned bushes, rather than shrubs – that show the tendency toward invalidism so characteristic of modern roses. If you grow a wide enough selection of roses, covering the history of the European rose, it will not be long before you find that everything dating from after the 'revolution' tends to suffer from blackspot, rust and other rose ailments far more than those that went before.

Nevertheless, the Hybrid Perpetuals, Hybrid Polyantha, Hybrid Tea and Floribunda roses that occupy the last few beds of this National Collection represent the height of floral beauty that man has been capable of achieving. That he has done so at the cost of the health of the plants and a constant preventative regime of spraying, is perhaps to be expected.

Among modern roses, only the so-called Hybrid Musks, raised mainly in the 1920s, retain real robustness of constitution. They were something of a dead end, however.

Not such a dead end is the development that the Botanic Garden at Birmingham does not demonstrate – yet. One feels that it cannot be long before the English roses, bred by David Austin, find their way into the National Collection of the History of the European Rose. Recognition in the rose world takes an unconscionably long time – understandably, one must admit – but it must eventually come to these superb shrub roses, in which the best modern colours and vigorous remontance are combined with the grace and captivating flower shapes of the Gallicas, Damasks and Albas of long ago. They are the next step in the history of the European rose, and effectively eliminate the hiatus between the ancient and the modern.

Roses in the National Collection of the History of the European Rose

It is salutary for English people to note the great preponderance of French names among roses up to the beginning of the twentieth century. Although the rose is always thought of as quintessentially English, historically it is much more a French flower than an English one. Lyons was the great centre of rose breeding and the first Hybrid Tea was raised by Guillot Fils of that city.

Many of the roses are hybrids whose make-up is more than likely to include 'blood' from other groups than the ones in which they are placed, but they are classified according to the

Above: **'La Ville de Bruxelles' a Damask of 1849.**

Below: **Rosa gallica complicata.**

Photos Bill Shaw.

hope that he will forgive me for correcting them. As a result of my own research, I have also added some dates that were absent.

Bed 1. *Rosa gallica*
    Charles de Mills
    Belle de Crecy (1848)
    Duchesse de Montebello (1829)
    Cardinal de Richelieu (1840)

Bed 2. *Rosa gallica*
    Versicolor (Rosa Mundi) (prior to 16th century)
    Empress Josephine (1853)
    Tuscany Superb (1848)
    Officinalis (The Apothecary's Rose)

Bed 3. *Rosa gallica*
    Duc de Guiche (1829)
    Jenny Duval. Regarded by some authorities as identical to Président de Sèze.
    Tricolore de Flandres (1846)
    President de Sèze (1836)
    Belle Isis (1845)
    D'Aguesseau (1823)

general characteristics of the groups to which they show most affinity, and with very few exceptions their placings in the categories are generally agreed among authorities.

Other than the dates, any comments are my own. Occasionally I have given dates different from those given by Professor Hawkes, in the

Bed 4. *Rosa gallica*
  Georges Vibert (1853)
  Duchesse d'Angoulème (1827)
  Gloire de France (1828)
  Du Mâitre d'Ecole (1840)

Bed 5. *Rosa damascena*
  Marie Louise (1813)
  Léda
  Celsiana (1750)
  Mme Hardy (1832)

Bed 6. *Rosa damascena*
  Ispahan (1832)
  Blush Damask
  Kazanlik
  La Ville de Bruxelles (1849)
  R. damascena versicolor (York & Lancaster.
    Before 1551)

Bed 7. *Rosa bifera*
  Quatre Saisons
  R. canina
  R. canina 'Froebelii'

Bed 8. *Rosa alba*
  Belle Amour. Found in a convent garden in
    France.
  Maiden's Blush (before 1738)
  R. alba semi-plena
  Amelia (1823)
  Celestial. Origin and date unknown.

Bed 9. *Rosa centifolia*
  Robert le Diable. Origin and date unknown.
  Blanchefleur (1835)
  Tour de Malakoff (1856)
  Juno (1847)

Bed 10. *Rosa alba*
  R. alba maxima
  Queen of Denmark (1816)
  Félicité Parmentier (1836)
  Mme Legras de St Germain (prior to 1848)

Bed 11. *Rosa Centifolia*
  La Noblesse (1856)
  Provence. A dubious name; *Rosa centifolia*
    was known as the Rose of Provence (not
    to be confused with the Provins Rose – a
    Gallica)
  Old Cabbage (1583). Probably better called
    'Centifolia'.
  Rose de Meaux (1789)
  R. centifolia cristata Also known as 'Cha-

peau de Napoléon' (prior to 1827).
Fantin Latour (date unknown; the artist's
  name is no guide)
R. centifolia bullata (before 1815).

Rosa gallica versicolor, **known as 'Rosa Mundi'.** Photo Bill Shaw.

**Bed 12. *Rosa centifolia muscosa* (Moss
  roses)**
  William Lobb (1855)
  Mareschal Davoust (1853)
  Gloire des Mousseux (1852)
  Blanche Moreau (1880)
  Nuits de Young (1852 in the Collection.
    Laffay, raiser of many Moss Roses,
    produced it in 1845)

Bed 13. *Rosa centifolia muscosa*
  Capitaine John Ingram (1856)
  Alfred de Dalmas (1855)
  Henri Martin (1863)
  Salet (1854)
  Duchesse de Verneuil (1856)

Bed 14. *Rosa centifolia muscosa*
  Louis Gimard (1877)
  Mme de la Roche-Lambert (1851)
  Old Pink Moss (1727)
  Lanei (1845)
  Jeanne de Montfort (1851)

***Rosa gallica officinalis*. The Apothecary's Rose or Red Rose of Lancaster.**
Photo Bill Shaw.

Bed 15. *Rosa chinensis*
Miss Lawrence. (the same as 'Miss Lowe'? Author's suggestion.)
Mutabilis (prior to 1896)
Hermosa (1840)

Old Blush (approximately 1790. Thought by some to be 'Parson's Pink China', but this cannot be determined)
Single Pink (from Reading University)

Bed 16. *Rosa chinensis*
Perle d'Or (1809)
Jenny Wren (1956). Note the modern date.
Cecile Brunner (1881)
Sophie's Perpetual. Origin and date uncertain.
Bloomfield Abundance (1920)

Bed 17. *Rosa bourbon*
Honorine de Brabant. Origin and date unknown.
Bourbon Queen (1835)
Boule de Neige (1867)
Mme Lauriol de Barny (1868)
Souvenir de la Malmaison (1842).
Variegata di Bologna (1909)

Bed 18. *Rosa bourbon*
Commandant Beaurepaire (1874)
Zigeuner Knabe (1909)
Mme Pierre Oger (1878)
Mme Isaac Pereire (1881)
Mme Ernst Calvat (1888)
La Reine Victoria (1872)
Louise Odier (1851)

'Hugh Dickson', a Hybrid Perpetual rose dating from 1904.
Photo Bill Shaw.

Bed 19. Hybrid Perpetuals (HP) and Portlands (P)

Ulrich Brunner (1881) HP
Gloire de Doucher (1865) HP
Ferdinand Pichard (1921) HP
Arthur de Sansal (1855) P
Jacques Cartier (1868) P
Comte de Chambord (1860) P
Mabel Morrison (1878) HP
Rose de Rescht P
The Portland Rose (prior to 1809) P

Bed 20. *Rosa foetida* and Noisettes

R. foetida 'Austrian Yellow'
R. foetida 'Austrian Copper' (1590)
R. foetida 'Persian Yellow' (1830)
R. noisettiana 2002 (from Reading University)
Mme Plantier (1835). Often listed as an Alba, although not a true one.
Céline Forestier (1842)
Irish Cluster
Blush Noisette (before 1817)
Jaune Desprez (Desprez à Fleurs Jaunes). The collection has the date as 1835, and other authorities cite 1830, but it would appear to have been raised by Desprez in 1826.
Mme Alfred Carriére (1879)

Bed 21. Hybrid Perpetuals

Général Jacqueminot (1853)
Baronne Prévost (1842)
Hugh Dickson (1904)
Georg Arends (1910)
Eugène Fürst (1875)
Baron Girod de l'Ain. The collection gives the date of this rose as 1868. It was, in fact, raised by Reverchon in 1897.
Paul Neyron (1869)
Empereur du Maroc (1858)

Bed 22. Hybrid Perpetuals

La Reine (1842)
Souvenir du Docteur Jamain (1865)
Frau Karl Druschki (1901)
Baroness Rothschild (1868)
Fisher Holmes (1865)
Reine des Violettes (1860). Not a Hybrid Perpetual, but almost always classified with them.
Mrs John Laing (1887)
Roger Lambelin (1890)

Bed 23. Tea Roses

Rosette Delizy (1922)
Marie van Houtte (1871)
Perle des Jardins (1874)
William R. Smith
Mme Bravy
Mme F. Kroger
Mme Wagram
Souvenir de P. Nabonnard
Lady Hillingdon (1910)
Devoniensis (1838)

Bed 24 is devoted to Hybrid Musk roses of the 1920s, Bed 25 to Hybrid Polyantha and *Rosa multiflora*, and Bed 26 to Dwarf Polyanthas. The first Hybrid Tea, 'La France', raised in 1867, leads off Bed 27, and from there until Bed 32, which examines the search for a blue rose in the years from 1957 to 1977, the collection traces the development of Hybrid Teas and Floribundas after World War 2, from 'Ena Harkness' and 'Frensham' (1946) to Cocker's 'Glenfiddich' of 1976.

Around the walls of the demonstration garden are *Rugosas, Spinosissimas, Eglanterias,* and many different kinds of climbing roses.

The White Rose of York - the Alba rose 'Semi Plena'.
Photo Bill Shaw.

Mottisfont Abbey:
Pre-1900 Shrub Roses

The collection of old roses at Mottisfont Abbey is in complete contrast to that at the University of Birmingham, although it spans the same groups of plants. The difference has to do with the purposes for which the collections were put together.

At Birmingham, as we have seen, the object is academic study. There is no question about the aesthetic effect of the roses on students, but they are not laid out to that end. Their arrangement in the *pulvulli* (the usual term 'Order beds' is inappropriate when all the plants belong to one genus) is designed to make it easier to appreciate the distinctions between the different kinds of roses and to form a mental picture of their development through time.

At Mottisfont, the purpose is to show old roses in a garden setting. There is nothing systematic about their layout, although occa-sionally roses of the same kind are grouped together for effect. The collection was made primarily by Graham Stuart Thomas, who searched for old roses for many years and whose contribution to their renaissance as garden plants has been immeasurably impor-tant.

Thomas was for many years Gardens Advi-sor to the National Trust. During his career and on into his retirement his presence has been an adornment to horticulture and his talents as painter, draughtsman, photographer – and above all as one of the most authoritative writers of his time on plants – have enhanced the knowledge and enjoyment of more than a generation of gardeners.

It was typical of the man to whom, it appears, the welfare of plants and their appreciation among gardeners are more important than

Below: **The vigorous 'Souvenir du Docteur Jamain', a strongly scented Hybrid Perpetual rose raised by Lacharme in 1865, seen at Mottisfont Abbey.**
Photo Bill Shaw.

Opposite, above: **Roses at Mottisfont: in the left foreground is the Scotch Rose hybrid, 'Stanwell Perpetual', of 1838. Photo Bill Shaw.**

Opposite, below: **Mottisfont Abbey. The beautiful and uncommon old rose 'Botzaris', a nineteenth-century Damask.**
Photo Bill Shaw.

other considerations, that he gave his entire collection to the National Trust. The story of the collection, of how Graham Thomas first encountered old roses in Ireland in the nineteen thirties, and of how his newly awakened fascination survived the war years and led to friendships with people whose names read like a twentieth century roll of gardening honour, is told in his book *The Old Shrub Roses* (Dent, 4th edition reprinted, 1980), which is mandatory reading for all who love these plants.

Meanwhile, the National Trust maintains the collection at Mottisfont and keeps it open to the public. A day out in the Hampshire countryside focused on Mottisfont takes you as close to the true heart of England and Englishness as it is possible to get. The setting is much the same as it must have been in 1201, when the Priory of the Holy Trinity was founded. Certainly it is little changed since the house was rebuilt in the first half of the 18th century,

From the house, smooth grass sweeps gently down to the tree-shadowed Test – the finest trout stream in Britain and as Mole and Ratty a river as it is possible to imagine. One waits in the summer stillness agog lest the Water Rat's little boat should appear round a bend with Mole manfully pulling the oars while Rat pits his considerable wit against a supper-bound fish.

On the way back from the river you pass the astonishing, crystal-clear spring, still pumping its massive 200 gallons a minute as when it first attracted the monks to the spot. All around are huge trees of which one, a double-trunked London plane, has the widest canopy of any tree in Britain.

The roses are at some distance from the house in a large, old, walled kitchen garden. The paths are edged with box and the design is geometrical, but it is not easy to discern this when the roses are in full fig at the height of summer. The season is short, as most of the roses flower but once, and amiable queues gather when the admission kiosk opens for the day. Many a lasting gardening acquaintanceship has been struck up while waiting to see the Mottisfont roses – it is that sort of occasion.

The impact of the roses is immediate and overwhelming, but there is no harsh brilliance of colour. Neither are the roses exhibited in platoons and squadrons like guardsmen on the sovereign's birthday. Instead there is a welcoming, warm lushness, a feast of colour that is easy on the eye, and a powerful but subtle

The White Rose of York in full fig at Mottisfont.
Photo Bill Shaw.

of box and in borders before the walls. The old brick walls themselves are clad in climbers and ramblers, beautifully trained on precisely tensioned wires. The standard of cultivation is simply superb and just what one would expect from a showplace of the National Trust.

You can come to Mottisfont just to absorb the atmosphere and let the roses work their magic upon you, but you are certain to take some ideas away with you as well as memories. That is part of the general idea. The collection is above all a garden, and the ways in which the roses associate with one another, with the double herbaceous border down the middle of the garden, and with the occasional discreet and perfectly matched under-planting, are as educational to the gardener as the academically arranged roses at Birmingham are to students of the history of the rose. If you can see both, you will find yourself enslaved for life by the magic of the old roses.

The day at Mottisfont has more to offer after you leave the abbey. Go to the village – it is hardly that – and enter the tiny post office. They provide cream teas of wondrous quality there, to be savoured slowly outside at rustic tables on the little village green beneath the most enormous and most fruitful walnut tree you are ever likely to see.

supremacy of scent. You should not, however, expect sugary romance. There is nothing cloying about the National Collection of Old Roses. Centuries of selection have not been spent to create vapid prettiness or unending essays on pink. There is strength enough to keep you enthralled for hours and to forbid you ever to forget your visit to this ultimate summer place.

There are over 300 different roses, with the shrub roses deployed in beds between the lines

Mottisfont Abbey. The rose on the wall in the fore- and middle-ground is the Noisette 'Mme Alfred Carrière', of 1879.
Photo Bill Shaw.

The Veitch Family Graves

The National Council for the Conservation of Plants and Gardens finds itself up against all sorts of constraints when trying to exercise that part of its remit that concerns gardens, as opposed purely to plants. The world is ever one in which power and influence, and the money that buys both, will almost always drive out idealism if it should get in the way.

Occasionally, however, there are happier stories to tell, and one of them concerns the Devon Group, the largest in the country, which has nearly 1200 members. They are an active, enthusiastic group, in a county that is noted for its gardens. It is not only noteworthy gardens open to the public such as Rosemoor (owned by the RHS), Killerton, Knightshayes, Marwood Hill, and the Garden House at Buckland Monachorum that make the reputation of the county; it is also, as any mail-order nurseryman will tell you, the quality of its private gardens, whether in town or country.

The status of Devon as a gardening county is in no small measure due to the enormous influence of one family of nurserymen, the House of Veitch. Their profound importance to British gardens cannot be exaggerated, and although the weight of their greatness was transferred to a large extent to London, Devon remained the heartland of the Veitch tradition. Their London nursery no longer exists, but the Exeter one does under the name of St Bridget's Nurseries. It is no longer owned by the family, but the present owners are extremely proud of the Veitch nursery heritage.

Among those who love plants, the Veitch name is particularly revered for the family's extraordinary activity in the field of plant collecting. Between the years 1840 and 1905, they despatched at the firm's expense no fewer than 22 collectors, including three members of the family, to practically every part of the globe where plants grow. Often suffering dreadfully from disease or injury, assailed by bandits, endangered by revolutions, attacked by wild animals, shipwrecked, stranded, exhausted, and in at least one case, tragically dying, the

The Veitch family graves, Broadclyst Parish Church yard, near Exeter.
Photo Mike Squires.

intrepid travellers sent back such a stream of plants that gardening was utterly transformed in those few years.

John Veitch was born in Jedburgh, Scotland, in 1752. He moved south as a very young man with ten shillings in his pocket and went to work for a London nursery firm for eight shillings a week. Before he was twenty years old he was commissioned by Sir Thomas Acland to lay out a park at Killerton in Devon, and in a very short time he was appointed agent for all the Acland estates. Eventually Sir Thomas actively encouraged John to set up a nursery of his own at Budlake, not far from Killerton. The nursery was in existence in 1800. In 1832, John and his son James, aged 40, bought land in Exeter to be nearer their market, and this was the founding of the Exeter nursery. It should be borne in mind that John was still running the firm at the age of eighty, and did so for another five years, before handing over the business to James. He died two years later, in 1839.

James and his son, also James, presided over a prospering business, now called James Veitch & Son, and they decided to expand, purchasing a nursery in Chelsea in 1853. James senior stayed in Exeter, while his son went to London. Later the firm split, the name going to the London operation. The Chelsea nursery became famous for orchids and greenhouse plants as the Royal Exotic Nursery, fed by new introductions from the firm's travellers in the tropics. At Coombe Wood, hardy trees and shrubs were grown, and these were also the main stock-in-trade of the Exeter firm.

The London firm closed down in 1914 after a glittering reign over the nursery world. In Exeter, however, Robert Veitch & Son continued its distinguished existence under Peter C.M. Veitch, the second member of the family to be awarded the Victoria medal of Honour of the RHS, and then finally the last member of the family to be in the business, Mildred Veitch, who sold it in 1969.

Camellia x *williamsii* **'Mildred Veitch'.** Photo Mike Squires.

Haglis Cottage, Killerton, first home of the Veitch family.
Photo Mike Squires.

During a relatively short period up to World War 1 – not much more than sixty years – a torrent of plants flooded into British gardens and completely transformed them, causing changes of style and emphasis that have led directly to the ways in which we garden today. To a very large extent, the House of Veitch was responsible for it.

During that sixty years, Veitch collectors introduced:-

118	exotic ferns
232	orchids
498	stove and greenhouse plants
49	conifers
72	evergreen and climbing plants
153	deciduous trees, shrubs and climbing plants
122	herbaceous plants
37	bulbous plants

John Veitch, the founder of the firm, is buried in the churchyard of Broadclyst Parish Church, just outside Exeter. Also interred there are his wife and son, James, and his family. Recently, two local people, Mike and Edna Squires, who are notable gardeners, were approached by a member of the Parochial Church Council who suggested that they might like to help 'to tidy up the graves'. Mike is chairman of the Devon NCCPG group, and Edna is group secretary, and it was not long before their committee had been approached and decided to give the Veitch graves the dignity they deserved.

The first step was literally to tidy the graves. They consist of a central interment chamber, along one side of which are five headstones. Buried there are:-

John Veitch, who died 22 November 1839 aged 87

Anna Veitch, wife of John, died 1 January 1809, aged 36

James Veitch, who died 14 May 1863, aged 70

Mary Veitch, wife of James Veitch, died 20 March 1825 (aged approximately 30)

Rebecca Veitch, second wife of James Veitch, died 8 May 1863, aged 65

Anna D. Veitch, daughter of James and Mary

Broadclyst Parish Church.
Photo Mike Squires.

Veitch, who died 26 February 1845, aged 21

William T. Veitch, son of James and Mary Veitch, who died 29 May 1847, aged 27

The inscriptions that give these dates hint at considerable family tragedy. John's young wife, Anna, was lost to him when he was 57. From James's date of birth one can infer that she was married when 19 or younger and John was about 40. She must have been well loved, as she is remembered in the name of her grand-daughter, Anna D. Veitch. James senior, we learn, lost his mother when he was sixteen.

James's first wife, Mary, died when they were both in their early thirties, and he then had the misfortune to lose two of his children in a little over two years in their young adulthood. It was indeed fortunate for him, and for the House of Veitch, that his two other sons, James junior and Robert, lived, the one to found the newly separated firm in London, and the other to carry on in Exeter.

It is thanks to the Devon Group that we are able to put the flesh of human interest on the bones of a family history that is usually re-counted in terms of the firm. But there is more to their endeavours than that.

The grave site itself, and a border that has been made nearby between two ancient yews, is now a memorial garden planted with trees, shrubs and perennials introduced to cultivation by the House of Veitch. The first plantings included:

Acer palmatum 'Dissectum Atropurpureum'
Camellia x *williamsii* 'Mildred Veitch'
Erica x *veitchii* 'Exeter'
Myrtus luma (syn. *M. apiculata*)
Gaultheria hookeri (syn. *G. veitchii*)
Gaultheria nummularioides
Corydalis wilsonii
Ourisea coccinea
Primula cockburniana
Dicentra macrantha
Acacia 'Exeter hybrid'
Berberidopsis corallina
Ceanothus x *veitchianus*
Tropaeolum speciosum
Rhododendron schlippenbachii

This last, the rhododendron, along with other woodland plants with a Veitch provenance, is to be planted where bays at one side of the church are north-facing, and where the church's previous efforts at gardening had proved abortive.

On a spring day in 1993, a century and a half after the death of John Veitch, members of the Devon Group, their friends, and visitors from far afield, gathered in the churchyard. In the church itself an exhibition had been mounted, featuring Veitch plants as cut material and potted specimens, and family memorabilia from the St Bridget's and Killerton estates.

After a brief opening ceremony for the new garden, a specimen magnolia was planted in the churchyard as a tribute to and in memory of those members of the Veitch family interred within it. The spirit of old John Veitch must indeed have been touched when the spade was put in the hands of the man who was to plant the tree. For it was none other than Sir John Acland, direct descendant of Sir Thomas, his employer and friend of so long ago.

Effigy of Lady Acland, wife of Sir John, in Broadclyst Parish Church.
Photo Mike Squires.

The Veitch Plant Collectors		
William Lobb	California and South America	1840-1857
Thomas Lobb	India and Malaya	1843-1860
Richard Pearce	Chile, Peru and Bolivia	1859-1866
John Gould Veitch	Japan, South Sea Islands, and Australia	1860-1870
David Bowman	Brazil	1866
Henry Hutton	Java and the Malay Archipelago	1866-1868
Carl Kramer	Japan and Costa Rica	1867-1868
Gottlieb Zahn	Central America	1869-1870
George Downton	Central and South America	1870-1873
J. Henry Chesterton	South America	1870-1878
A.R. Endres	Costa Rica	1871-1873
Gustave Wallis	Brazil, New Granada, Tropical South America	1872-1874
Walter Davis	South America	1873-1876
Peter C.M. Veitch	Australia, South Sea Islands, and Borneo	1875-1878
Guillaume Kalbreyer	West coast of Africa, Colombia, South America	1876-1881
Christopher Mudd	South Africa	1877
F.W. Burbridge	Borneo	1877-1878
Charles Maries	Japan and China	1877-1879
Charles Curtis	Madagascar, Borneo, Sumatra, Java and the Moluccas	1878-1884
David Burle	East Indies, Burma and Colombia	1881-1897
James H. Veitch	India, Malaysia, Japan, Korea, Australia and New Zealand	1891-1893
E.H. Wilson	Central & Western China and the Tibetan frontier	1899-1905

Leeds Castle Foundation:
Monarda and Nepeta

Leeds Castle is utterly romantic. It sits on an island in a small lake in Kent, and its walls rise sheer from the water. The oldest part of the castle, the Keep, first built fifty years after the Norman conquest, has its foundations below water level and is connected to the rest of the castle by the double arch of a two-storey bridge. Venice's Bridge of Sighs is a backstreet afterthought by comparison.

Few castles of such age, built above all else for security, can have proved so effective in that respect over such a long period of time as Leeds has. Before the conquest, Earl Godwin, who knew a defensible spot when he saw one, was in occupation, and in 1978 Cyrus Vance, Moshe Dayan and Egypt's Mohammed Ibrahim Kamel met at Leeds Castle for Middle East peace talks.

To read the roll of owners of the castle is to touch the heart of Britain's history. Its first Norman owner, before building in stone commenced, was both Earl of Kent and Bishop of Bayeux. It was home to Eleanor of Castile, she of the Charing (*chère reine*) Cross, and for almost 300 years thereafter the property of royalty. From 1552 to 1974 it was privately owned, notably by the families of St Leger, Culpeper, Fairfax and Wykeham-Martin. Now it

is owned by the Foundation set up by its last private owner, Lady Baillie, and is a major tourist attraction.

On the mainland, as it were, a short distance from the castle itself, is a range of low buildings that includes the estate office and the gift shop. Behind them is the Culpeper Garden, named after the family who owned Leeds Castle from 1632 to 1710. Nicholas Culpeper, the seventeenth century herbalist, whose book of herbal remedies is on many a gardener's bookshelf today, was a kinsman.

The Leeds Castle brochure says that Nicholas Culpeper would have been pleased by the recent addition of a herb border along one wall, but that is to miss the point, because the garden is planted in the style of an old English cottage garden, and that is what would truly gladden the heart of the old boy were he able to return to see it.

The Culpeper Garden is in fact modern, and was created in 1980 by the celebrated garden designer, Russell Page, whose book, *The Education of a Gardener,* is now a classic. In it he tells of his dawning passion for plants as a boy in Lincolnshire in the early years of the century, and how every plant he set his heart on seemed only to be found in 'cottage gardens in hamlets lost among the fields and woods'. The cottagers would give him cuttings from plants that were not to be found in any catalogues, and he says, '...here was a whole world of modest flower addicts'.

He is talking of an era long before the NCCPG and National Collections were ever heard of, and yet what could be more in the spirit of today's conservation of garden plants? Tucked away in their country fastnesses, rural gardeners kept the old favourites going, many of which we cherish today and keep track of with computers.

It is fitting that there should be two National Collections of cottagey plants in the Culpeper Garden. *Nepetas,* which include the well-known catmint, are found throughout the temperate parts of the northern hemisphere. *Monardas* are American, but put them among old pinks,

The very rare *Monarda stipitoglandulosa.*
Photo R. Ward.

A mixture of monardas.
Photo Thompson & Morgan.

lupins, mulleins and other traditional English garden plants and they fit in as to the cottage born. *M. fistulosa*, one of the two principal garden species, was introduced from Virginia as long ago as 1656, so its presence here is entirely appropriate. This species has been known as bergamot, or even wild bergamot, since the nineteenth century, the name having previously belonged to the lemon mint.

The other species that figures prominently in the garden hybrids is *M. didyma*, known as Oswego tea, because its leaves were used to make a hot drink, much appreciated in the frigid winters of Oswego County, on the Lake Ontario shore of Upper New York State. It has pink flowers and needs a moist soil, whereas *M. fistulosa* has purple flowers and tolerates dryness much better. This correlation between colour and moisture requirements runs in the hybrids as well.

The range of colours of the two genera – mainly lavender and mauve in *Nepeta*, purple to pink and light red in *Monarda*, fits in perfectly with the palette with which the Culpeper Garden has been planted. It is an enclosed garden, with the old estate buildings on three sides and the third side looking over the lower part of the small lake which, in the true tradition of modesty so dear to the hearts of British landowners, is called the Great Water.

The beds are edged with low box hedges and there are brick and stone pathways between them, the whole garden giving an impression of one luxuriant drift of softly toned, scented flowers.

The man in charge is Mr Bristow, the grounds manager and head gardener, but the collections are looked after under his guidance principally by Chris Skinner, assisted by Richard Ward.

Chris hopes that before long the collections will have their own bed. At the moment they are rather fragmented, largely because there have been so many recent additions that they have had to be scattered about rather than brought together in one place. Nevertheless, serious enquirers are shown round the collections and time is taken to talk and to give all the information they may require. As Chris says, 'They are given their own private guided tour'. This happens ten to fifteen times a year, and on top of that there are numerous telephone enquiries. Chris and Richard also attend NCCPG plant shows and those put on by the Hardy Plant Society, at which many more contacts are made. They can also sell surplus plants there,

the proceeds from which are used to purchase items needed for the collections. These may include, for example, books necessary for identifying species that, because of their scarcity in cultivation, do not appear in the more general garden literature.

Chris Skinner finds the problem of naming a frustrating one, but then we all do. It is a constant thorn in the collective flesh of National Collection holders. Frankly, if in some cases it is not, then the job is not being done properly, as it is fatal to be complacent about the identity of cultivars and ignorant to dismiss the shifting sands of botanical science as merely faddish.

As an employee of the Leeds Castle Foundation, one might expect a less than ultra-long-term perspective in the collections from Chris. On the contrary, however, he visualises their development over decades, rather than years, and would like to see them become significant educational tools for colleges and individual students. This sense of responsibility is typical of the young professional gardeners of today. They may move on, but they see the nation's gardens as comprising one large firm, among whose departments their careers may cause

Monarda 'Ou Charm'.
Photo R. Ward

Far left: **Monarda citriodora.**
Photo R. Ward.

Left: **Nepeta 'Snowflake'.**
Photo R. Ward.

them to move, but whose overall welfare is of the first importance.

It is also indicative of a proper sense of proportion and modesty when such dedication is shown towards just two not greatly distinguished genera among so many. *Nepeta* consists of low, drought-resistant plants of subdued colouring and has the disadvantage of there being something intrinsically comical about plants that induce ecstasy in cats that roll on them. Nevertheless, the grey-leaved, bushy *N.* x *faasenii* is an extremely popular garden plant, and the much larger 'Six Hills Giant' is a valued item in borders, especially where the climate is too cold or damp for the sun-loving *N.* x *faasenii*.

You might think that that was all there was to the genus, but you would be mistaken. *N. govaniana*, which likes to grow where it is cool and moist, is one of the longer-flowering plants of summer, producing spikes of yellow – not the usual mauve – on plants of 90cm (3ft) in height. *Nepeta nepetella* is a Pink Sheet plant (see p36) that is slowly becoming available to gardeners and is in the lists of three nurseries, one of which is the Monksilver Nursery, whose activities are described on p 32.

One of the most encouraging aspects of the National Collections at Leeds Castle is that they are thriving, and so is the garden in which they are to be found, at a time when, as at Dyffryn (p 110), economic pressures have taken their toll of ornamental horticulture on the old landed estates. It is sad to see vital windbreaks cut down to make room for tawdry gift shops, garden staff cut below the minimum needed for proper maintenance, and important plants jettisoned because they lack 'visitor appeal'. Leeds Castle has attracted attention for its successful and enlightened management, which does not find it necessary to follow the short-sighted, quick-return ideas of other establishments, where terms such as 'visitor spend' curdle the milk of quality.

We owe earlier generations of owners of great houses an enormous debt for their sponsorship of plant collectors and the nurseries that sent them to the furthest corners of the world. We are greatly obliged, too, to the cottage gardeners of rural Britain for their conservation of garden plants. There was a great deal of traffic in plants between the two, and the significance of Leeds is that the connection between castle and cottage is being maintained, and not sacrificed on the altar of the bottom line.

Tom La Dell: **Arbutus unedo**

The distribution of certain plants from the warmer tips of the British Isles to Portugal and adjacent parts of Spain is one of the more intriguing and even romantic aspects of the British and Irish flora. As one whose education was scientific, I hesitate to say that thoughts of Atlantis come to mind, but they do – and I take some comfort from Mr and Mrs D.F. Maxwell who, finding outstanding specimens of the Cornish heath, *Erica vagans*, on Goonhilly Down while on their honeymoon in the 1920s, named one of them 'Lyonesse', the Cornish name for the legendary drowned land between Iberia and Britain.

If you take a map of the Western Approaches and Spain and imagine you have made a loop of thread with the power to lengthen itself at your will, mentally cast it so that it encloses Portugal, the north-west corner of Spain and a little of Spain just east of Portugal, the tip of Cornwall, West Cork, Kerry, Clare and the Connemara. In doing so you will have envisioned an outline of the area of the Lusitanian flora (Lusitania was the Roman imperial province which included Portugal and part of Spain in the time of Augustus Caesar). If you use your thread loop to enclose the area of distribution of individual plants, it will sometimes shrink to define a little of the Iberian peninsula, while on other occasions it will expand to clip Cornwall's toe or encompass Ireland's prime tourist area. Now and then it will balloon eastward, taking in the Mediterranean basin or parts of the alpine chain. Never, though, does it more than flirt with the British Isles.

In the south-west and west of Ireland there is a remarkable population of native wild plants that is like no other in the world. It is a crossroads of botanical history, where the northern extremes of the sub-tropical flora meet the

The garden at Muckross House, in the Killarney National Park.
Photo John Kelly.

southernmost reaches of arctic plant life, and where relics from the ice ages, such as the spring gentian (*Gentiana verna*), grow innocently by the roadside, unmolested and unsullied by litter. Your loop would have to extend beyond Lusitania to include Savoy, part of Switzerland, mountainous areas of northern Spain, and Counties Cork and Kerry to delineate the native area of the greater butterwort (*Pinguicula grandiflora*), whose blue-purple flowers, twice as large as any other species, stand above its fly-paper foliage. It would shrink again to define the natural home of St Dabeoc's heath (*Daboecia cantabrica*), a heather from County Galway and just the north-west rim of Iberia. Shorten it even more and it will ring the Portuguese and Irish distributions of *Saxifraga spathularis*, the St Patrick's Cabbage that is hugely prolific in Cork and Kerry – and absent from the rest of the British Isles. Fling it wider, embracing the shores of the Mediterranean as far as what we once knew as Jugoslavia, and just reaching the mountains and lakes around Killarney, and you describe the timeless haunts of *Arbutus unedo*, the Irish strawberry tree.

It is an unusual plant in many ways. It is usually more of a shrub than a tree, not often reaching much more than 6m (20ft), and less than half that on the Dalmatian coast. It is an ericaceous plant, part of the largely lime-hating heather and rhododendron family, yet it will grow on chalk. Its flowers, typically urn-shaped like so many of the ericaceae, have fruits that are hugely untypical and look for all the world like those of *Cornus kousa* or, indeed, strawberries.

It does not end there, for this handsome evergreen flowers in autumn at exactly the same time as the fruits from the previous year's flowers are ripening. Catch it in late October and you will see the red fruits and white flowers together, beautifully set off against the mid-green of the leaves. It has few close relatives: there are only two other species in cultivation. One, with which it hybridises in the wild in Greece, is from the eastern Mediterranean, while the other comes from an area extending from British Columbia to San Francisco. This last, *Arbutus menziesii*, is a noble tree, up to 18m (60ft) high in cultivation, with smooth, terracotta branches of exceptional beauty. Other species, from further south in California and Mexico, are not hardy enough for our gardens, but it is interesting to know of the existence of such as *AA. xalapensis, arizonica and texana*,

if only so that we can marvel at the aeons of time that separate the Irish and Mexican descendants of common ancestors.

Come down to earth now and put away your loop of definition. The next stage in this story (for that it what it is) is a nursery in Kent. It is not a glossily packaged garden centre, but a working production unit producing plants for a landscaping business. Its owner is Tom La Dell.

Tom is a refreshing character. He obtained his MA from Oxford University, his subject being the pure science of botany, specifically genetics, but he is no dry academic. His analytical mind sweeps away irrelevancies and unclear thinking, and he applies it to himself as well as the world around him. He was, for example, on the threshold of working on plant breeding at the Caribbean Botanic Garden in Kingston, Jamaica, until he realised that his own character and the inherent slowness of plant breeding were probably incompatible.

Arbutus unedo colonising cliffs on the shore of the Upper Lake above Killarney. Photo John Kelly.

Killarney Upper Lake with *Arbutus unedo*.

Photo John Kelly.

He turned to landscaping and put himself through two years of solid practical experience working on a nursery, in a botanical garden, and for a landscape contractor, before building up his own thriving business. Currently he is setting up a landscaping master plan for the Brogdale Horticultural Trust at Faversham, where the public will be able to walk round and learn about the history of fruit cultivation world-wide. It is planned that there should be a version of the Garden of the Oranges in Cordoba and one of the Versailles fruit garden, as well as truly authentic Chinese and Japanese fruit gardens. All this is highly relevant to the main subject of this book, as it is at Brogdale that you will find the National Collections of apples, pears, plums, cherries and cobnuts that are among the most important of all.

Tom holds the National Collection of *Arbutus unedo*. Sometimes it is a little difficult to understand how an apparently tiny group of plants can justify the title, but this collection is an object lesson in how much each of us who might take that view has to learn. I have to confess that, having grown the strawberry tree for many years, I had no idea of its having more than one variant – until I met Tom.

There seem in fact to be about eight. One is quite widely in cultivation. This is *A.u.* 'Rubra', which is very variable and has flowers that are anything from some shade of pink, or just flushed with pink, to red, although the latter are hard to find. Pink forms occur among the wild Irish population. There is a specimen with deep pink flowers at Glasnevin, the Irish National Botanic Garden, but most others are on the pale side. The name should probably be correctly written as *Arbutus unedo* forma *rubra*.

'Elfin King' is also firmly in cultivation. It arose on a Californian nursery as a sport on 'Compacta'. 'Elfin King' is a bushy form of the species, eventually of medium size, but with the advantage of flowering and fruiting while still quite small.

'Compacta' is described in Bean's *Trees and Shrubs Hardy in the British Isles* as 'A dwarf bush that does not flower freely'. It is thought, certainly by Tom, to be lost to cultivation and its place to have been taken by a plant, introduced from the New Zealand nursery of Duncan & Davies, that flowers beautifully when still young. This is the plant to expect if you see the label 'Compacta' on plants for sale.

Typical specimens of the species have toothed leaves, but in *A.u.* forma *integerrima* they are entire (smooth-edged). The one in cultivation represents other similar forms in the wild as Tom has seen them in southern Spain, and is slow growing and not generous with its flowers. 'Quercifolia', which one or two nurseries list, is, by contrast, oak-leaved. *A.u.* forma *myrtifolia*, sometimes referred to as 'Myrtifolia', has small, myrtle-like leaves and is not readily found in cultivation.

One or two of the variants have been found by Tom, much to his surprise, as he had thought them extinct. John Bond, supervisor of the Savill Garden in Windsor Great Park, and one of Britain's finest plantsmen, told him of 'Merriott', a compact variety named by the nursery firm of Scotts, of Merriott in Somerset, which had been propagated at the Savill. Later, he discovered 'Plena', a form highly desirable for its flowers but, because of its doubleness, unable to produce fruit.

In Ireland, *Arbutus unedo* grows wild on the banks of Killarney's lakes and on islands in them, and at the edges of old woodland. It is a light-demanding plant and will not grow deep in the woods. A geological fault, running through the enormous wild park, separates the old sandstones from the limestones, and the strawberry trees can be found growing equally happily on both. The species, including forma *rubra*, used be found during the last century in the vicinity of Glengarriff, just in County Cork at the head of Bantry Bay and not far from Garinish Island, and there are a few wild specimens of the species left there. There is very little variation in the wild population in Ireland today. Typically, populations do vary, but the range of the Irish plants was drastically reduced during the 19th century, when the country, once densely forested, was denuded of timber for fuel, building, shipping and smelting. *Arbutus unedo* once grew plentifully over much of the peninsulas of Beara and Iveragh and the south-west in general, and one must suppose that then there was considerable variation.

Today, unheeding tourists in their thousands every year drive within a few yards – sometimes literally inches – of one group of the strawberry trees that grow on the banks of Killarney's famous lakes. There are a few hundred within quite a small area, and they include many small seedlings, as well as the largest and tallest of all the Irish strawberry trees, a giant of 15m (50ft) or so. There are grounds for thinking that this biggest Irish specimen is very likely to be the tallest in existence anywhere. This noble, gnarled, ancient tree looks for all the world like one of the evergreen oaks, such as *Quercus ilex*. If you climb or scramble down to this particular lake shore – it is slippery, precipitous and dangerous – you can see tough, twisted specimens growing out of the living rock, and the birds twitter among them in late autumn as they gorge on the ripe, red fruits. Perhaps here, at last, is some wild variation, as one of the trees is a week or so later in flower than usual.

The scene is now finally set for the climax of this story. The Irish National Parks Department

The habitat of *Arbutus unedo*, with MacGillicuddy's Reeks, Ireland's highest mountains, in the background. Photo John Kelly.

Right: **Probably the largest specimen of *Arbutus unedo* in the world, over twice the height of any in cultivation. Wild in Killarney National Park.**
Photo John Kelly.

Below: **Tom La Dell in his nursery in Kent, with young specimens of varieties of the Killarney Strawberry Tree.**
Photo John Kelly.

runs the superb garden at Muckross House, just outside Killarney town and alongside Muckross Lake. It also looks after the wild stands of *Arbutus unedo,* among other things ensuring that they do not become overwhelmed by the blitzkrieg currently being mounted by seedlings of *Rhododendron ponticum.* Tom has been in touch with Cormac Foley, the National Park's horticulturist, and as a result the garden at Muckross will receive from him a full set of varieties of the strawberry tree. There is no question of their being planted in the wild – that would be wrong – but within the boundaries of the same National Park, future generations of Irish people, as well as the visitors from all over the world who flock to Killarney every year, will be able to see the full range of forms taken by the Irish strawberry tree – thanks to a man from Kent with a refreshing view of life's priorities.

Jeremy Wood: **Helleborus**

There is something about hellebores that nudges the superstitious side of some people and tries to awaken the fears of the 'Bastard Black Hellebor' that used to lurk in the days before modern science. On the other hand they are capable of captivating gardeners to an extent not commonly seen. It is not quite a question of either loving or hating them; some people exhibit towards hellebores merely a cool indifference.

Infusions of hellebore roots used to be given against insanity. In Gerard's *Herbal* of 1597, 'A purgation...is good for mad and furious men, for melancholy, dull and heavie persons...troubled by black choler and molested with melancholy'. Today, melancholy people do not enjoy hellebores, perhaps because of their sombre colouring and a waxy texture to the flowers that conjures some shuddering allusion to the art of the embalmer,

while those of more cheerful, though still sensitive mien, find them deeply alluring. I have observed that indifference to them is mostly to be found among spirits governed by common sense and practical tendencies.

They are adornments in the garden in winter and early spring, especially when grown among shrubs and in shady places. Hellebore foliage is varied, but always handsome and decorative long after the flowers are over. They are relatives of the buttercups, and the flowers are similarly saucer-shaped and rounded but much larger and have a colour range from almost black to pure white. The dark pigments are purples and deep purple-reds, which are streaked, stippled, lightly brushed or flushed on to a ground colour of sallow cream. In some species they are absent, leaving a field of white or light green, while in others they may appear as picoteed edgings to the petals.

Helleborus '**Citron**'. Photo Neil Campbell-Sharp.

Above: **Helleborus 'Capricornus'.**
Photo Neil Campbell-Sharp.

Right: **An Eric Smith hellebore hybrid.**
Photo Neil Campbell-Sharp.

Hellebores do not mind whether the soil is alkaline or acid, but it just so happens that the National Hellebore Collection is in a deep, medium loam that is just on the acid side of neutral. The postal address is Salisbury, which might very well lead you to expect the chalk downland of Wiltshire, but in fact Jeremy Wood's one-acre garden is only just in that county and is more akin to Hampshire's acid, New Forest soils. It misses the chalk by the skin of its teeth. The name of the village – Whiteparish – suggests a chalky outlook and indeed the same Salisbury to Romsey road that bisects the triangle of village green with its neat, cottagey, red-brick houses, skirts the side of Pepperpot Hill, a renowned chalk viewpoint just under two miles away.

The nature of the garden is reflected in Jeremy's always having been a member of the Hampshire Group of the NCCPG, and the collection actually belongs to the group. When he retired, his experience with hellebores was recognised by his being asked to co-ordinate the collection. He does not grow all the plants; they are shared between his and five other gardens within the group, but to him falls the task of looking after and keeping up the entry book, card index and photographic library.

From the outset, the policy has been to include species as well as cultivars. Some authorities have strongly put forward the view that National Collections should confine themselves to cultivars while leaving it to the botanic gardens of academic institutions to concern themselves with species. It seemed pointless to the group to collect cultivars without the species they were descended from, and their opinion makes a great deal of sense when it is remembered that the collections should be available for study. It is of as little use to a student of cultivars to have no species material to hand as it would be for someone studying the character development of the British people to know nothing of Celts, Romans, Saxons, Danes and Normans.

Not all the cultivars in the collection are named. A cultivar does not become such by being named; it has a perfectly legitimate existence without a name being published. One vital function a National Collection can perform is to give unbiased trials to cultivars so that the rush into publication, seen to such deleterious effect in *Hosta* and *Camellia*, among others, may be avoided. The best hellebore breeders are noteworthy for the great care with

which they avoid naming cultivars unless they are so outstanding that they really must be named, and the National Collection reflects and encourages this.

At a meeting of the Kent Group of the Hardy Plant Society, I looked at an exhibit mounted by Elizabeth Strangman, the well-known nurserywoman and plantswoman. It consisted of hellebore flowers, every one of which was different and none of which was anything less than first class. Very few had names. This deep sense of responsibility comes over every time one has contact with hellebore people, and it is an example that should be held high in the horticultural world.

The vast majority of named hellebore cultivars are derived to some extent from *Helleborus orientalis*, the Lenten rose. This is now taken to include the subspecies *abschasicus*, *guttatus*, and *olympicus*. Also included are early flowering plants under the name of *H.o. Kochii*

Top: **Helleborus x nigericors.**
Photo Neil Campbell-Sharp.

Above: **Helleborus x nigristern.**
Photo Neil Campbell-Sharp.

**One of Elizabeth
Strangman's
hellebore hybrids.**
Photo Neil
Campbell-Sharp.

Group, and plum coloured ones that appear usually as *H. atrorubens* of gardens. 'Of gardens' in this sort of context means a name with no botanical standing but traditional among gardeners.

These various cadets provide flowers that are all-over dark, ruby purple, marked with that colour as described previously, tinted with rose, green, or rich cream, or (and) speckled and spotted with maroon in varying degrees of density. The Kochii group are distinct, whatever their origin. Not only do they flower early, but their ground colour is distinctly yellow, rather than cream, and their leaves are larger than usual and markedly toothed.

Lent is a movable feast, and so is the flowering time of the Lenten rose. You can have these hellebores in flower any time from the new year to early April, and it is an excellent idea to make your own small collection of them so that together they have a season of a few weeks. When I was a head gardener, I made the mistake of planting too many of one sort, so that, although the display was by no means short, it was not what it could have been.

There are about fifty named cultivars in the collection with *H. orientalis* in their parentage. It looks as though there are something like thirty in general cultivation, almost all of which are only individually obtainable from one of about six nurseries offering them. Your corner nursery or garden centre is likely to provide seedlings or mixed divisions, but highly unlikely to have named forms. Indeed, divisions are less likely than seedlings, as hellebores hate being disturbed – the main reason why there are so few named cultivars in commerce. This is a field in which there is a classic role for the NCCPG and the National Collection scheme to play, as all the pressures are towards the

Helleborus **'Philip Ballard'.**
Photo Neil Campbell-Sharp.

neglect and eventual disappearance of cultivars.

The most famed seedling of all is, or was, 'Ballard's Black'. This was raised at Colwall, Malvern, at the old Ballard Nursery, now owned by Paul Picton (see p.115). It is believed no longer to exist, and Graham Stuart Thomas is of the opinion (his opinions are to be taken with the greatest respect) that all plants under its name are merely seedlings. Meanwhile, Mrs Helen Ballard has continued, elsewhere in Worcestershire, prolifically to produce hybrids, using *H. purpurascens* to induce very dark, blackish colours. Among the few of her named, dark hellebores are 'Blue Spray', which is blue-purple, and 'Philip Ballard', blackish purple. Her other target is a true lemon yellow, and she has considered 'Citron' to be good enough for release, although it is not yet in commerce. Her example is perhaps what inspires other raisers of hellebores to show restraint in naming and distributing cultivars.

'Pluto', 'Capricornus' and 'Cosmos' are hybrids raised by the late Eric Smith. They descend in part from *H. torquatus*, which is notable for passing on speckling to its offspring, and none of them is in the trade. Once again, they are preserved from the fate that befell 'Ballard's Black', but would almost certainly be destined to disappear for ever were it not for the NCCPG.

Jeremy Wood himself displays the extraordinary modesty that pervades the world of hellebore breeders. Although the National Collection includes a number of seedlings that he has raised, he has only ever considered one to be truly worthy of being added to the list of named hellebores. It is called 'Pearl', and one hopes that it will be a permanent addition to our garden flora.

Elizabeth Strangman is unique in the nursery trade. There is an unfortunate spirit of venality abroad among nurserymen today. It is by no means universal, but is firmly entrenched in certain establishments, and plants with known and serious defects are often bruited about as the best thing since the black tulip. Miss Strangman has produced many unnamed hybrids without trying to capitalise on them, including outstanding yellows and dark purples that would make lesser mortals hear cash register bells ringing a full peal of grandsire triples. She has also studied hellebores in the wild. In particular, she has introduced double forms of the Balkan *H. torquatus.* One cultivar that she has named is, Jeremy says, in a category of its own. It is called 'Violetta' and has purple edging and streaking on a white background.

The collection also includes hybrids made in a different area of the genus. Robin White, a nurseryman from Alresford, Hampshire, is noted for his crosses using the Christmas rose, *Helleborus niger.* This plant is not the easiest to please and does not always flower at Christmas, but when well suited selected forms of it produce enormous, round, pure white flowers of great beauty.

Crosses between *H. niger* and *H. corsicus* have been made several times since the first crossing in 1938, which produced *H.* x *nigericors.* The flowers are greenish white and borne in clusters against the dark green foliage, but both the colour and quality of the flowers as well as the depth of green in the leaf vary, and improvements are what growers like Robin White aand Miss Strangman are looking for. *Helleborus* x *nigristern* (*H. niger* x *sternii*) was originally produced by Eric Smith, and work on that cross continues quietly.

This is one of the most impressive fields of endeavour in modern ornamental horticulture. If yours is a character with a certain leaning towards Eeyore, you may find hellebores less than jolly, but no matter whether you enjoy them or view them with indifference, you cannot be other than deeply respectful of the way in which those who are associated with the National Collection of this unusual genus – co-ordinated, it may be noted, by an amateur – go about its affairs.

Helleborus lividus.
Photo Neil Campbell-Sharp.

Houghall College:
Meconopsis

Houghall is the Durham College of Agriculture and Horticulture. It is typical of many county colleges of its type; indispensable to the farming community, remarkable for the dedication of staff, and given to providing a deeper, more rounded finish to pupils than one might at first credit. Young men and women sometimes enter county agricultural and horticultural colleges with academic certificates that are not particularly wide-ranging, but almost always leave as articulate, informed, competent, culturally enriched people.

Sport plays a proper part in their lives, as befits students of such physically demanding disciplines. I first came to know Houghall College during the early 1960s, when living and working in Durham City. The rugby football team invited me – a referee and ex-player – to become their unofficial coach, and for two seasons we had some quite notable successes so that it was with sadness that I left to found a nursery in the Midlands.

The college has moved on over the years and what was then the rugby pitch is now given over to golf greens. Thirty years ago little more than a start had been made on the development of the 10 hectares of grounds into sports fields and ornamental features, within which is now one of the largest collections of hardy plants in the north-east of England.

Houghall has one of the best gardens in the north, too. There is a large water garden, where *Hosta, Salix, Iris* and *Primula* thrive and help to provide a wildlife habitat where spring sees frogs, toads and newts happily breeding. There is an alpine house; and rock gardens, raised beds and troughs are planted with a wide range of species with an emphasis on *Fritillaria, Lewisia* and *Cyclamen*. In spring, the gardens are ablaze with the thousands of daffodils and narcissi that are naturalised under trees, and a large heather garden, providing colour all year round, has been developed and planted by the students. What is arguably the best feature of all is the arboretum, where more than 300 different trees, including the National Collection of *Sorbus* (mountain ash and whitebeams) can be seen.

There are rose gardens, shrub borders, a wild flower meadow, herbaceous borders and seasonal bedding displays. For those who study at the college, whether students preparing for their full-time careers or just amateur gardeners taking a lesson a week, there is an opportunity to feel a sense of belonging to a future 'Great Garden'.

It is surprising how many Great Gardens have been made in unpromising sites, largely because it was not good economics to build your house on land good enough to earn its living. Houghall has its share of disadvantages.

A dwarf form of the variable *Meconopsis napaulensis.*
Photo J.M. Hirst.

***Meconopsis napaulensis,* the Satin Poppy, may be red, purple, or purple-blue, rarely white, and even more rarely yellow.**
Photo J.M. Hirst.

Life in the north-east is often bitterly cold. Blizzards as early as 1 November are by no means unknown, vicious, razor-edged winds howl in from the east, and the frost pocket in which the garden sits annually records some of the lowest temperatures in the country.

The soil, however, is a mixed blessing. It is a light, sandy, acid loam – the sort of soil informed gardeners dream about because, although it requires very large annual dressings of bulky organic matter, if these are given generously the horizons of gardening widen sharply and the grinding labour involved in, say, heavy clay, is not incurred.

Hence the success of the woodland garden, originally consisting of trees planted as a windbreak, and now a home from home to rhododendrons, primulas, lilies, and many other aristocratic denizens of a lime-free, woodland environment. Here is to be found the jewel in Houghall's crown, the National Collection of *Meconopsis*, a genus for which Houghall's organically fed soil is ideal.

Meconopsis is the genus to which the fabled blue poppies of the Himalayas belong. Other species may have red, yellow, or white flowers, but it is the blue ones with which the generic name is synonymous in the minds of gardeners. Unfortunately, this state of affairs is in the process of change.

The only species outside the Sino-Himalayan massif is the yellow-flowered *Meconopsis cambrica* known as the Welsh poppy. It is a native of Europe and occurs in the more mountainous parts of Great Britain, where it may sometimes be seen growing by the roadside. This is the species to which the name *Meconopsis* was first given, and it constitutes what is known as the 'type' species. Current research points strongly towards its being separated from the rest of the genus, and the rules – formulated in the *International Code of Botanical Nomencalature* – decree that what will happen then is that the name will be retained by the Welsh poppy, while the rest will have to be found another. In other words, the blue poppies and their ilk will no longer be *Meconopsis*.

Botany does not have an enviable reputation when it comes to re-christening genera. The ghastly example of the metamorphosis of *Cornus canadensis* into *Chamaepericlymenum canadense* is an ever-present warning of the fact that the authors of botanical names have failed to follow the mellifluous examples set by

Linnaeus and his successors. Lewis Carroll would have enjoyed the manufacture of portmanteau words in botanical Latin in which are celebrated such things as the branching of the stigma (*Dicranostigma*) or the fact that the unfortunate plants have conspicuous bracts (*Megaskepasma*). However, in the case of *Meconopsis* – which means 'looks like a poppy' – a euphonic solution is at hand which, with the greatest diffidence, I put forward here. If the one species in *Cathcartia* could be renamed, it would leave its generic name free for much more distinguished plants. Maximowicz originally placed the lovely, yellow-flowered *M. integrifolia* in *Cathcartia* after its discovery by Przewalski (of Przewalski's Horse) in 1872, and it would be hard to find a more pleasant-sounding 'off the peg' name for the new genus.

Unfortunately, *Cathcartia villosa* appears to have been named first, so the rules, framed for just the sorts of complications that would arise

Meconopsis integrifolia was one of the new plants collected by E.H. (Chinese) Wilson on his second trip for Veitch (1903-5) to Western China (see page 69).
Photo J.M. Hirst.

if *Meconopsis villosa* were to become a species of *Cathcartia*, seem to prohibit such a solution. However, the rules are flexible, and one might hope that a monotypic genus (only one species) might be able to bow before one with almost fifty. There is another solution; in cases where names are universally held in affection, they are occasionally allowed to stand. It would be a pleasant use of this prerogative if it could possibly be interpreted to allow a re-allocation of the Welsh poppy while permitting the rest of *Meconopsis* to stay put. Currently the front runner for the new generic name is *Meconanthon*, which has two disadvantages. One is that the specific epithets will have to change gender from feminine to neuter, so that *Meconopsis villosa* would become *Meconanthon villosum*; the other is that it is just plain dull and sounds more appropriate for a collection of Asimovian humanoid robots than a genus of breathtakingly beautiful plants.

I have gone into this fairly deeply with more than one motive. Partly it is to show that the naming of plants is not an easy matter for the botanists, and in no small measure to plead for euphony in naming. Also it is to demonstrate that you have to have your wits about you if you are a National Collection holder. With one of the principles being that interested parties should be able to visit the collection for the

purposes of study, it helps if you are aware of whether the genus consists of 45 species or just one.

Houghall currently holds twenty species. There are, however, 63 different 'labels', representing collections from different sources in the wild, botanical varieties, hybrids and forms of hybrids. One of the species, *M. henricii*, is as far as I can see only in cultivation at all because of its being collected in the wild by Mike Hirst, Houghall lecturer and curator of the collection, who found it on the Gongga Shan (Minya Konka), a mountain in the west of the Sichuan Province of China that was once thought to be the highest in the world. In fact it is a shade under 25,000ft at 7,590m. While admittedly *Meconopsis henricii* does not grow at such dizzy altitudes on the mountain, but at around 4500m (15,000ft) on nearby slopes, Mike's expedition must rank with the most dedicated exploits connected with the National Collections.

As this is written, *Meconopsis* is still the accepted name for these wonderful plants, so it is used here for all of them – both the perennials and the monocarpic species. Monocarpism is displayed by plants that die after flowering and setting seed only once. They are not the same as biennials, which make their growth one year and then flower, set seed

Meconopsis x beamishii is the name for hybrids between *M. grandis* and *M. integrifolia*.
Photo J.M. Hirst.

Both left:
Meconosis dhwojii is a monocarpic perennial from Nepal.
Photo J.M. Hirst.

and die the next. Monocarpic plants may take several years to build up their substance before flowering in a final burst of energy that, with seeding, is their last act.

Some of the perennials are more perennially-inclined than others. The most popular and well known of the blue poppies, *M. betonicifolia*, is likely to die if its first attempt at flowering is allowed to succeed. Incipient flowering stems should be removed in the first year so that the plant's energy is diverted into growth. Thereafter, it should be reliably perennial.

M. betonicifolia is not at all difficult to grow and is a good border plant in cool, moist climates with soils that are neutral to acid and well laced with fibrous organic matter. The flowers in such situations will be a good, pure blue, with several on each 1.2m (4ft) stem. The warmer and drier the climate and the limier the soil, the more the flower takes on a washed-out mauve colouring, until the conditions become too extreme for it and it will not grow at all.

The most stunning of the blue poppies species is *M. grandis*. It can be from 90cm to 1.5m (3-5ft) tall, and carries huge flowers, each on a long stalk. They have four petals and in the best forms the stalks arch over so that the flowers look downwards to resemble pure blue Tiffany lampshades. Houghall have about a dozen forms of this magnificent species,

including the form under Sherriff's collection number GS 600, which is known as the 'swan-necked grandis'. It ranges in the wild through Nepal, Sikkim and Tibet and into China and is one of nature's most spectacular gifts to our gardens.

Meconopsis have a predilection towards hybridising, and *M. grandis* has to be carefully pollinated if it is to breed true. Crossed with *M. betonicifolia*, it shows great hybrid vigour in producing the largest and most imposing meconopsis of all, *M. x sheldonii* 'Branklyn'. Its colour is, however, on the muddy side, with quite a lot of purple in the blue. 'Branklyn' is not present in the Houghall collection at the time of writing, but half a dozen other forms are, including 'Slieve Donard' – named for a famous Northern Ireland nursery – and 'Ormswell', raised in Scotland and, like many of the collection, contributed by Jim Jermyns. Jim is the proprietor of the Edrom nurseries in the south of Scotland, and is proving to be a worthy successor to Alex Duguid and the Misses Logan Home, three unassuming but magnificently eccentric characters to whom the world of cool climate alpine and woodland plants owes a great debt.

The term 'Lampshade Poppy' is sometimes applied to the yellow-flowered *M. integrifolia*, a plant rendered spectacular, not so much by its size – it is only 30cm (12in) high – as by its

Right: **Meconopsis horridula var rudis.**
Photo J.M. Hirst.

Far right: **Meconopsis horridula at 16,000 ft in the Gongga Shan (Minya Konka), a range of mountains in western Sichuan province, China.**
Photo J.M. Hirst.

Below right: **M. henrici in the Gongga Shan.**
Photo J.M. Hirst.

Below, far right: **The most famed and most widely grown species is M. betonicifolia.**
Photo J.M. Hirst.

enormous flowers, which can be 15cm (6in) across. It is another denizen of West Sichuan, where *M. henricii* and the strangely bristled *M. horridula* are also found. It is monocarpic, and this factor tends to reduce its popularity with non-specialist gardeners.

What a shame this is! Gardeners above all other folk should surely be possessed of patience. Still, if they are not, they can enjoy the hybrids of this beautiful species with the blue poppies. They are perennials, and the blue colouring turns out to be recessive, so that cream and yellow dominate to the exclusion of blue and purple save for markings on the petals. Houghall have the very rare *M. x beamishii*, which is *M. integrifolia* crossed with *M. grandis* and has light, creamy yellow flowers. In *M. x sarsonsii* the other parent is *M. betonicifolia* and the hybrid is a steady, reliable garden plant.

Reliability is the keynote of M. *napaulensis*, the queen of the monocarpic meconopsis and quite capable of making flower spikes 1.8m (6ft) high in red, yellow, white or shades of blue and purple. Its leaf rosettes are worth growing for themselves alone. Indeed, most meconopsis have handsome foliage, sometimes lobed, sometimes not, and anything from velvety-downy to the sort of bristles that might deter any but the most hungry donkey. It is not hard to grow and thrives on cool, moist, leafy soils everywhere in the British Isles. One of the most beautiful plants I have ever seen was a cherry-red form of this species, flowering regally in a garden at a place in Scotland called Achnashellach, somewhere in the hills above Kyle of Lochalsh, where it rains like nowhere else on earth and the slaty rubble that passes for soil supports a clamorous and joyful population of fat primulas, stately meconopsis and mighty gunnera. When I was there the garden was awash and the West Highland midges attacked like shoals of poisonous, aerial sharks. It was all worth it just to see this one plant, tall and serene, right

Himalayan blue poppies; *Meconopsis betonicifolia.* Photo J.M. Hirst.

royally bedecked in scarlet and scornfully bidding the dreadful weather to do its worst.

The inimitable *M. wallichii*, a fountain of white poppies and quite unlike any other plant, is held by some to be a form of *M. napaulensis.* Who cares? Well, the botanists do, and Mike Hirst and others at Houghall have to care as well. As for us gardeners, let us wish them well with the naming changes to come. They will probably not be the last. What matters above all else is that these supremely wonderful plants are being assiduously looked after in a Durham garden where continuity of the collection is as assured as it is possible to be. Meconopsis are not all woodland plants. Some grow in nature on open moorland, while others live on windswept screes at high altitude. All their natural habitats are under environmental stresses that hardly bear thinking about, as deforestation leads to more of their their top-soil being swept into the Bay of Bengal each year and these lovers of coolness and moisture face environmental changes that are quantitatively uncertain but inevitable for all that.

A very fine form of *Meconopsis grandis* raised at the Edrom Nurseries, Coldingham, Berwickshire.
Photo J.M. Hirst.

Kenneth Adlam: **Ferns**

Ferns are strange, but beautiful plants. They are of unbelievably ancient descent, long antedating the first flowering plants. Ferns appeared about 100 million years before the dinosaurs, long before the first reptiles, and at about the same time as amphibians. When ferns were well established, the first insects began to make their appearance.

They do not flower or set seed, but reproduce in a way that suited an insectless, damp continent (there was only one then; Pangea had not yet split into the continents as we now know them). The fern plant has two phases. One is the structure we recognise as a fern; the other is a tiny, green, scaly, hermaphrodite flake that bears sex organs of both kinds and becomes pregnant with a new fern which grows to maturity and then develops, usually on the backs of its fronds, spore-bearing organs. These, when ripe, drop enormous numbers of tiny spores to the ground, where they develop into reproductive flakes once again. This fascinating process is known to botanists as the 'Alternation of Generations'.

The male cells swim across the surface of the flake to reach the female ones. For this to happen there must be an unbroken film of moisture. In the late Devonian and the Carboniferous ages, when ferns developed, the climate of Pangea was warm and wet. The plants had a long period of settled conditions in which to become the dominant vegetation, and ferns with huge fronds or with thick, tall trunks like trees luxuriated in the muggy fogs.

As man himself may well find out before he is much older, things change. The world became drier, continents broke off from Pangea and travelled about, creeping slowly into positions where they experienced cold, drought, excessive heat and tearing winds. Ferns re-

A maidenhair fern from the Himalaya, *Adiantum venustum*, quite at home in Ottery St. Mary.
Photo John Kelly.

The rusty-back fern, *Ceterach officinarum*, wild in the Burren, County Clare, Ireland.
Photo John Kelly.

treated as only those small enough to huddle away from the threatening conditions, or those lucky enough to sail on continents where ferny conditions were maintained, survived.

Now there are tree ferns, but they are confined to the tropics and sub-tropics. One or two are from temperate parts of Australasia and can be grown in places like Cornwall and the southern parts of Ireland as woods through which you can walk beneath the much-divided fronds. In the tropics there are ferns with frond-spans of 9m (30ft), and the atmosphere is moist enough for others to grow on trees without the benefit of roots or soil. In the British Isles, some ferns still show a love of the epiphytic way of life, growing in the leaf mould lodged in the forks of old trees, or even colonising old roofs.

In the National Collection of Ferns – that part of it held by Kenneth Adlam – there are representatives of the tropical ferns. You will not find *Angiopteris evecta*, the largest non-tree-fern in the world, but a stagshorn fern, *Platycerium bifurcatum*, hangs from the ridge of his greenhouse, its flat, branched fronds

persuaded that it is at home. It is an Australasian species, from warm temperate regions, but its close relatives are almost all tropical.

Kenneth lives in Devon but is no stranger to hotter climates. He spent many years in India and has grown exotic plants in places that to you or me sound romantic. However, one suspects that the commercial cultivation of groundnuts may have had its less glamorous moments. Kenneth and his wondrously hospitable wife Dolsheen, retired to what is by any standard a romantic part of England. Sadly, Mrs Adlam passed away while this book was in production.

Would you not love to live in a place called Ottery St Mary? It is a small town, but the modern world seems to have passed it by. In fact, it literally has, as the two main roads that thunder with holiday traffic, cursing and jostling towards Torquay, Padstow and Penzance, run to either side of it. The only access to the town is by lanes as narrow and twisting as when the horse and cart you are half expecting to meet was the pride and joy of the local haulier.

It is woodsy and closely hilly. Leaving the narrow streets of the town behind, your lane plunges into old trees with mossy north sides. It twists and dips like a gentle roller-coaster, and here and there houses sit back and relax. All along the laneside banks there are ferns. Not bracken – ferns. Ferns that believe themselves back in the dreamtime of the old continent, moist and content.

One of the houses is Kenneth's, and around it is a paradise for ferns. The area is right, the climate is almost perfect, and there are few people who can match his skill with them.

Kenneth is at least a third-generation lover of ferns. His grandfather had a superb collection of forms of *Asplenium scolopendrium*, the hart's tongue fern, and his father grew and was interested in all ferns, including tropical ones, which had their own greenhouse.

He is first and foremost a gardener, not a botanist, although his botanical knowledge is considerable. He recalls his father and one of the great figures of horticulture of the earlier part of this century, A.J. Macself, discussing the British Pteridological Society (ferns, that is) and refraining from joining because of the bias towards botany that they saw as too strong. The atmosphere of gardeners versus botanists persists in the society to this day, and it is only recently that a motion to change its name to The British Fern Society was defeated – admittedly by a small majority.

Horticulture is plagued by those whose vanity is to raise a superstructure of academicism over it. It is, I am certain, in no small measure due to this that ferns are generally uncommon as garden plants. The names given to them before the international rules became more enlightened were enough to put anyone off. *Phyllitis scolopendrium fimbriatum drummondiae* or *Polystichum aculeatum pulcherrimum gracillimum* tempt the modern eye and ear to level allegations of downright élitism or exclusivity at the very least.

For anyone to fulfil the criteria of a National Collection of ferns, they must not only be expert at their cultivation, they must also be fitted to disentangle the valid names from the spurious and pretentious. It is not necessary to be able to construe Virgil or to quote chunks of Cicero at his most tedious. It is not incumbent on a gardener, either, that he be able to discourse upon cytotypes or apogamous complexes. Such things may be left to the profession of botany. Nonetheless, a fern collection makes its own special demands, not the least of which is an ability to discount the pseudo-academic and unravel pomposity.

Kenneth Adlam is not pompous. His is the approach of someone who loves plants, particularly ferns, and is content to apply his undoubted scholarship towards making them as accessible as possible as garden plants. He is as careful as possible about the correctness of their names, and studies quietly to that end, but he is always glad when they are validly simplified. He welcomes any reduction in heavy Latin, but treats what remains with the proper respect due to the tools of knowledge.

His collection is of hardy ferns. The tender ones in his greenhouse are not part of it, although they are very important to him. Of the hardy ones he has 'About 300 recognisable species together with 50 or so garden hybrids – some good, some awful'. To him all ferns are

Below: **Onoclea sensibilis, the American oak fern.**
Photo John Kelly.

Bottom:
Dryopteris affinis 'Cristata The King', a crested form of the golden-scaled male fern.
Photo John Kelly.

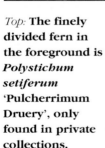

Top: **The finely divided fern in the foreground is** *Polystichum setiferum* **'Pulcherrimum Druery', only found in private collections.**
Photo John Kelly.

Above: **Tripinnate fronds of a member of the Divisilobum Group of** *Polystichum setiferum*, **the soft shield fern.**
Photo John Kelly.

of interest and importance, with the exception of one or two that he regards as freaks. 'As far as beauty goes', he says, 'the genus *Polystichum*' (the shield ferns) 'may win by a short pinnule'.

A pinnule is a sub-sub-division of a fern frond. The featheriness of ferns is expressed in the ways in which the fronds are divided. Hart's tongues and bird's nest ferns have undivided, strap-shaped fronds. Polypodies are pinnate – they are once divided, the divisions being called pinnae, from the Latin *pinna*, a feather. In other species, such as the male ferns, the pinnae are themselves divided. In such cases the divisions of the pinnae are called pinnules (little feathers). In some ferns the pinnules are divided not just once more, but twice, and the result is fronds that are quadripinnate – the ferniest ferns of all, among which are some of the shield ferns.

A whole vocabulary has arisen with which to describe the structures of different fern fronds. Words like 'plumose' and 'ramose' have distinct and proper meanings. However, they are of no concern to those of us who would like merely

to get to know ferns and to exploit their beauty in the garden.

One of the best ways of doing this is to grow them among other plants, rather than to try to emulate the Victorians whose craze for ferns resulted in grotesque ferneries and the eventual abandoning of the fashion. Kenneth's garden is an object lesson in how to do this, from the aesthetic point of view as well as the horticultural.

From him you learn that ferns lend an entire extra dimension to a grouping of plants. It is analogous to the presence of dainty foliage in a flower arrangement, although in the case of ferns they complement the foliage that already exists. Very little in the plant world can compare with the filigree of their fronds or the shiny straps with which the hart's tongue can carpet the ground among shrubs.

They obtain from their neighbours the part shade and protection from wind that they must have. Mere good gardening will provide them with the leafy, rich, moisture retentive soil that they need. Given such congenial conditions

Opposite, right: **A crested lady fern, *Athyrium filix-femina* 'Frizelliae Capitatum'.**
Photo John Kelly.

Left: ***Platycerium* sp. This stag's horn fern is not part of the National Collection, but Kenneth Adlam grows tender ferns for the sheer love of them.**
Photo Nicola Kelly.

**The National
Collection of tree
ferns is in Glasgow.**
Photo John Kelly.

Dryopteris affinis
**'Cristata
Angustata' in leafy
company.**
Photo John Kelly.

there are countless plant associations in which they can take part with telling effect.

As the Himalayan blue poppies rise up for flowering in late spring, so the croziers of the lady fern emerge and uncurl, until the blue lampshades of the *Meconopsis* open, perfectly displayed against the delicate tracery of green fern.

Small relatives of the hart's tongue unfurl their glossy, wavy, undivided fronds among pink-flowered *Erodiums*, little relations of the cranesbills (geraniums), in a plot so small that there is no garden in the country in which a similar effect could not be created. Ferns are not exclusive to the élite and the clever; they are simple plants for any gardeners who can spend a few moments in making a note of what their uncomplicated requirements are.

Many of the National Collections are in commercial hands, and most of them are none the worse for it. Kenneth Adlam's fern collection is, however, a prime example of the informed, skilled, reliable amateur upon whom the NCCPG and its plant conservation programme will eventually come to have depended.

His views on the conservation of plants and on the NCCPG and its National Collections are trenchant and concerned, but he himself is a collection holder upon whom others could with advantage model themselves.

Charis Ward and Sarah Sage:
Euphorbia and Sedum

Charis Ward and Sarah Sage live at Abbey Dore. It is quintessential England, found down a roly-poly lane and alongside a Wind-in-the-Willows river. The house and its attendant courtyard – a quadrangle surrounded by outbuildings – is of the stuff that that the postcards are made of that find themselves fondly displayed in places like Sanpete, Utah and Grind Stone City, Michigan.

All is not quite as it seems, though. Just down the road is the border between Herefordshire and Wales, so just how English is Abbey Dore? The River Dore would not appeal at all to the Water Rat were he to find his home under several feet of water in winter, as the river floods fairly drastically.

And the quiet Sarah Sage, efficiently running her gift shop or keeping a watching brief over the plants, is not just an expert gardener. She was famous as Sarah Ward (she is Charis's daughter), the international show jumper who, in the days when Colonel Harry Llewellyn was

chef d'equipe, carried off trophies for Great Britain from all over Europe and beyond.

Thus it was that there were fifteen horses in the party that came to Abbey Dore to live in 1967. There was also a herd of Jersey cows and five dogs. The place was a wilderness of bindweed and ground elder, flooded lawns, outbuildings in no fit state for the animals, and a nasty habit among the alder population of seeding itself everywhere.

The two women describe themselves endearingly as mad as hatters. In reality they are people for whom hard work and dedication come naturally. They are perfectly capable of conceiving a vision that nobody else would think remotely possible and then making it come true.

They named the River Walk while it was still head high in brambles and nettles and hidden by over a hundred saplings of alder and ash. Friends were roped in to help; sometimes they knew what was coming, sometimes not. One,

Abbey Dore Court.
Photo John Kelly.

whose dearest love is to relax with paints and easel, finished a weekend in a state of complete exhaustion mixed with happy fulfilment. He now tries to visit when there are projects to be admired, rather than tackled, but can never be certain.

By 1983 the number of visitors to the garden had risen to the extent that Abbey Dore was a going concern as a garden open to the public. There are not many like it, where the owners have created a garden from scratch that will sustain the interest of knowledgeable people, where well grown plants are for sale, and where there is other entertainment, entirely in character.

You can have tea at Abbey Dore, in one of the most charming tea rooms in the country. It was converted by Sarah from a stable, and the quality of the cream teas and imaginative snack dishes is extremely high. The service is gentle and attentive and entirely in keeping with the general atmosphere. Many of Sarah's international rosettes are on display, along with por-

traits of her favourite horses, and here and there the odd teddy bear peeps out at you.

If the family (or just you!) want to see teddy bears of every kind consorting together in large numbers, the gallery over the gift shop is a most satisfactory affair. At Abbey Dore you cannot have your plants in isolation; the place is to be savoured as a whole, garden, cream tea, bears and all. 'Mad as a hatter' is neither appropriate nor accurate; Abbey Dore is pure English eccentricity – warm, charming, and eminently sensible.

Tony Lowe of the NCCPG visited Abbey Dore in 1985. The two extraordinary women were at the time actually running a dairy farm as well as the garden, and had not been able to give quite as much attention to the plants as they could have wished. Nevertheless, Lowe immediately saw the potential of their cottagey style of gardening and had no hesitation in setting out to persuade them to take on two National Collections – *Euphorbia* and part of *Sedum*. They share *Euphorbia* with the Univer-

Sedums and euphorbias make good neighbours.
Photo John Kelly.

sity of Oxford Botanic Garden, something they regard with modesty but without being in the least intimidated.

It is not easy to carve out from the enormous genus *Euphorbia* just those which can be regarded as hardy in the British Isles. *Euphorbias* range from vicously thorny, cactus-like desert plants – the Crown of Thorns 'cactus' is a euphorbia – to non-succulent shrubs. On the equator in East Africa there are stands of euphorbias like candelabras made out of 9m (30ft) organ pipes – always in semi-desert and taken by most people for cacti. In complete contrast, the Irish Spurge, brilliant by the roadsides of Cork and Kerry in May, with its apple-green, 7cm (3in) leaves and ripe-lime flowers, revels in the wet, and the wood spurge faces stoically up to whatever an English winter throws at it.

Euphorbia mellifera, a shrubby spurge from the mist-wrapped laurel forests of the Canary Isles, grows well in Cornwall and parts of Devon, and survives most winters in parts of Dorset. It is, therefore, strictly speaking hardy in the British Isles. Does that mean that in order for a collection of euphorbias to be compre-

hensive it must be sited in one of those areas?

The exigencies of the practical world mean that comprehensiveness is sometimes an ideal that has to remain unfulfilled. However, it makes a good deal of sense to have the collection in a part of the country where it is warmer and sunnier than average, as euphorbias as a whole do like a decent summer. The Irish Spurge, just to be different, doesn't care about such things as long as its feet are moist. What to include in the National Collection at Abbey Dore turns out to be, like most gardening solutions, a matter of common sense, and you will find there a representative collection of the spurges that are most reliable in British gardens, along with some of the rarer and more desirable cultivars.

These plants all have narrow leaves that crowd closely on the stems, often arranged so as to be reminiscent of flue-brushes. The flowers are of no account, but are surrounded by bracts which are usually yellow or some shade of lime. Garden euphorbias are grown as much for the architecture of their stems and often evergreen foliage as for their flower bracts, even though the latter habitually last for many

**Abbey Dore;
euphorbias.**
Photo John Kelly.

weeks. To see the different kinds growing together at Abbey Dore is to appreciate just how much euphorbias can contribute to the character and interest of a border.

The same can be said of sedums. *Sedum* is another genus consisting mainly of succulent plants, and it is also a huge one with a wild distribution all over the northern hemisphere. Once again, a judgement had to be made as to which species could be accommodated at Abbey Dore, and a sensible restriction to a handful of species, those that perform best in garden borders (as opposed to rock gardens and so on), was made.

Sedums, such as *SS. maximum, spectabile, telephium*, and their hybrids and cultivars, are not of as great an architectural value as euphorbias, but share something of their appeal. Their rôle is to enhance the ripe tones of autumn and late summer, with wide, cushiony heads of tiny, close-packed flowers in shades of purplish pink to chocolate brown.

Sedum spectabile itself is a little obstreperous in its colour – described by Graham Stuart Thomas, who has visited Abbey Dore and rendered advice drawn from his vast knowledge and experience with the National Trust – as puce. Crossed with *S. telephium*, its choleric appearance is toned down to a proper pink, which later turns to a deep, bronze-red. 'Autumn Joy' is the best known form of the hybrid, but it is sterile and does not attract butterflies

with the magnetism that so distinguishes *S. spectabile*.

Forms of *S. telephium*, of which 'Abbey Dore' is an excellent example, have heads of flowers in which chocolate is mixed with a hint of red. Near white colchicums or the short-stemmed *Leucanthemum* x *superbum* 'Snowcap', their colour can be repeated with *Cosmos atrosanguineus*, which is also in flower late in the year and which completes the illusion by wafting a distinct scent of Bourneville on the air.

The leucanthemum was, until recently, *Chrysanthemum maximum*, but *Chrysanthemum* is now a rump genus consisting chiefly of weeds, while what the world recognises as 'chrysanths' are to be found shamefacedly lined up behind the ill-conceived name *Dendranthema* – a word that sounds more as if it defined the feelings of someone with a loathing of trees.

Sedum, too, is under attack from the botanical wordsmiths. Do you have a label long enough upon which to inscribe the legend *Sedum kamtschaticum floriferum* 'Weihenstephaner Gold'? And what do you think of the tautological *S. kamtschaticum kamtschaticum*? The wren used once to be *Troglodytes troglodytes troglodytes,* until somewhere the third hole-in-the-ground epithet was dropped. Let us hope botany is not about to descend into similar double tautology, because people like Charis Ward and Sarah Sage will be unable to get anything done for laughing.

Anne Stevens:
Trollius and Lobelia

Dorset is a benign county that can never quite make up its mind about whether it belongs to the South Coast or the West Country. Either provenance makes it a magnet for tourists and holidaymakers, although it is not sufficiently westward to avoid being a county that many people pass through without stopping.

Whether you stay or go, however, its rolling countryside cannot fail to impress. At the eastern end are the flatter undulations of the old heathlands, where purple rhododendrons line the roads in June. Further west come the chalk downs with the burial mounds of the Iron Age studding the crests of their curves. If you turn away from the arterial roads, you find networks of sleepy lanes linking hamlets with ancient names like Cheselbourne and Melcombe's Bingham. They run in deep folds of the coun-

Trollius **'Commander in Chief**'.
Photo Alan Stevens.

tryside, usually where trickling streams ('piddles' in the old speech; 'puddles' to the prissy Victorians) idly connect chalky fields with loamy, leafy hollows.

Not far from the Piddle Valley, Piddletrenthide, Puddletown, and Tolpuddle, where the Martyrs held their defiant meeting, is such a hollow. It has its own, reliable piddle and the soil is acid, so that rhododendrons and azaleas thrive in the shade of its trees. There is a beetle-browed thatched cottage beside it, surrounded by a garden that combines perfection of the cottage style with the firmness of design that comes from a rigorously artistic eye. This is the home of Anne Stevens, whose status as a plantswoman is evident at every turn.

Anne is an amateur gardener with professional connections. Ask her about her background and she says, 'I've always been a gardener'. She has wanted to garden ever since she can remember, and that goes back to when she grew radishes, spring onions and candytuft in her own part of her parents' garden in Barnes, near London, when she was six. Her uncle worked for a seed firm, and he and his Essex garden had a great influence on her, so much so that when she left school she went to work for Harrods' nursery in Barnes and gained, during the five years she was there, a grounding that has stood her in good stead ever since.

In everything she does, she is supported by her husband, Alan, a consulting design engineer whose studio is alongside the garden. His orderly mind takes care of the photography and garden records, and he can sometimes be found indulging in recreational weeding.

Somehow Anne manages to fit horticultural journalism and lecturing into her life, along with sitting on the committee that advises a television company on gardening programmes. The garden is open to the public on occasion, but there is also a constant stream of visitors of varying degrees of distinction in the gardening world for whom Anne's garden is irresistible.

To those who would say that the holding of a National Collection is too much trouble in lives already full of commitment, Anne's looking after two is sufficient answer. Her shady,

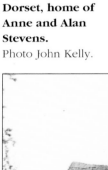

Ivy Cottage, Ansty, Dorset, home of Anne and Alan Stevens.
Photo John Kelly.

moist garden with its acid soil offers the perfect conditions for *Trollius* (the globe flowers), and for the moisture-loving *Lobelia cardinalis* and *L. fulgens.*

From the entrance gate, on a bend in the narrow lane, two broad borders curve sweetly between grass walks down to the stream and pond. They are packed with plants, yet each poppy and delphinium, every lupin and hosta has room to grow and contribute its own character to the harmonious whole. The cottage is hung with honeysuckle, clematis and banksian rose, and below it the dell is aflame in spring with deciduous azaleas. The dazzling red of 'Hotspur', matched closely with another of soft orange, demonstrate how correct tonal order makes for harmony where otherwise there would be a clash. Nearby, the yellow azalea (*Rhododendron luteum*), scents the air for yards around with a perfume of restrained headiness. It is quiet, sheltered, and only the small rush of water over the little dam below the pond disturbs the silence.

Trollius fit perfectly into the garden, not only because of the conditions, but also because the style of planting suits them. They are rather like very large buttercups, usually single in the species, but globe-shaped with incurved petals in *T. europaeus* - a British native – and especially the hybrids derived from it by breeding with species from Asia and China.

These vary from the rather delicate, ivory-cream 'Alabaster' and the pale yellow 'Canary Bird' to orange-yellow, as in 'Orange Princess' and the true orange of 'Salamander'. The flowers range from 2.5cm (1in) across to more than double that, and make a fine show, like upright, globular Chinese lanterns on their 60cm (2ft) stems.

Varieties of *T. chinensis* are of a different flower type. The outer petals form a cup-shaped ring, within which is a mass of petaloid stamens. The best known is 'Golden Queen', a well-established garden favourite, but the New Zealand-raised 'Imperial Orange' is beginning to arrive in general cultivation.

T. chinensis itself comes from remote parts of north China, near the border with Korea, where it varies from light orange-yellow to orange and grows in moist soil alongside the shuttlecock fern, *Matteuccia struthiopteris.* Botanists are still undecided whether it should in fact be called *T. chinensis* at all. Hitherto it has been known mostly as *T. ledebourii*, and this gives rise to the sort of dilemma that

Trollius yunnanensis. Photo Alan Stevens.

holders of National Collections, as well as other interested gardeners, find themselves up against.

Even if for no other reason than that you do not want constantly to be having to make new labels, changes in the scientific names of plants can be, to say the least, maddening. However, the botanists who decree them are, on the whole, reasonable people. What in fact they do, in common with all scientists, is to erect hypotheses about names, which other scientists are welcome to knock down if they can. In other words, they express an opinion about the place a plant holds in the world of plants, based on the best information available to them.

There being few facts in the world, but many changing viewpoints as new discoveries are made (chromosome science, for example, has revolutionised botany), most names are matters of opinion. What is important is how authoritative the opinions are. The name that emerges at the top of the pile will be the one that *for the*

Lobelia tupa, the most magnificent of the lobelias, growing about 15 miles from Ansty. It does not have a place in a National Collection. Photo John Kelly.

moment is backed by the preponderance of authoritative opinion.

With *Trollius chinensis* there are two problems for Anne Stevens as National Collection holder. The first is to decide which way to jump, as it were, as regards its name. The second is that it is not entirely certain that the plants in cultivation under either name really belong to the true, wild species at all. The first problem is solved by her following the balance of opinion and also by being prepared to change if necessary at a later date; the second is not hers to solve but is up to the scientists.

National Collection holders who do not keep up with the names of plants eventually devalue their collections and reduce their worth to those who want to study them. It also defeats the whole object if labels get switched and plants go out to other gardeners under false colours. The responsibility taken is considerable, and the rest of us gardeners should not forget the debt we owe to people like Anne and Alan, whose time and care goes into making as sure as possible that we find ourselves growing the right plants.

The same sort of problem attends Anne's other collection, that of *Lobelia cardinalis* and *L. fulgens.* So much hybridising has gone on with these sumptuous, 90cm (3ft) red beauties, that it is fairly pointless to try to unravel their breeding.

'Eulalia Berridge', for instance, occurred before World War 2 in the wonderfully mild garden at Anne's Grove, at Castletownroche, County Cork, Ireland. There is nothing in the British Isles more exactly like a sub-tropical river valley than Anne's Grove, and plants grow with a sensual abandon rarely seen elsewhere. The brilliant red of this lobelia is tempered by an overlay of mauve, and you could speculate all day about its antecedents, quoting at least four, and possibly five species. Who cares? In gardening terms the task is to keep 'Eulalia Berridge' true to name, not her parents.

These lobelias are as far removed from the blue bedding lobelia as you can get. They are not all that hardy, and it is as well to mulch them in winter even in mild places. Their real enemy is fluctuating temperature and drought, and in Anne Stevens' garden there is little of either.

New additions to the collections arrive all the time, either as seed or from nursery catalogues, or frequently as plants brought by friends from abroad. The collection is partly shared, but Anne believes that the larger collections *must* be shared or otherwise split up. She points out that anything can happen – an extreme rarity can be dug up by a badger just as easily as a plant that is in every garden centre, and a falling tree can cause untold damage.

She and Alan feel happily confident in the long-term benefit of the work they do with these two genera. In the event one day of their being no longer able to look after them, they know that the NCCPG would see to their care and that someone, somewhere, would have the right conditions. Meanwhile, however, they are in the best of hands.

Pat and Philip Vlasto: *Salvia*

The village of Child Okeford is not very far along the lanes from where Anne and Alan Stevens live, although you have to know your way. It should take you half as long as the main road by Blandford Forum, but is unlikely to if you take a wrong turning in this deepest, most secret part of England.

Philip Vlasto's retirement from medicine was not enough at first to persuade him and his wife Pat to withdraw from the bustle of Weymouth, and Pat's inner dynamo was geared to a faster pace than is to be found in the ancient valleys of north Dorset. She is a passionate gardener, devoted to plants, and of the sort that believes in joining in with a view to doing, as opposed to merely talking.

It was somehow inevitable, then, that when the first ever county group of the NCCPG started in Dorset, Pat would be in at the beginning. She saw clearly the most effective way of acquiring the information that was needed and became the group's collator, gathering and processing data on the county's stock of garden plants and passing it back to headquarters.

Naturally, she pursued the question of National Collections and, bearing in mind the mild climate of the county, particularly near the sea, encouraged among others the creation of the National Collection of *Salvia*.

Salvias belong to a huge genus, with species, including the kitchen sage, to be found all over the world. The flowers are often very brightly coloured in fine reds and true blues, with vivid purple and clear pink occurring frequently. They are sometimes in tight, long, conical spikes, and quite often they are relatively large and borne individually at intervals up the stem. Some are shrubs, others sub-shrubs (in which much of the stem dies back to a woody base), and still others are herbaceous, dying away entirely in winter. A few are annuals.

With such a wide distribution you would expect plants of varying hardiness, and sure enough species vary from bone hardy to requiring a heated greenhouse. Many, however, are on the borderline of hardiness in the southern parts of the British Isles, although they tend to resent the dampness of the milder parts of Ireland. For most of us, a few salvias add extra brightness to summer and autumn; a representative National Collection is a major undertaking.

The question is often asked, what happens if a National Collection gets into trouble? What if circumstances cause its dispersal or the collection holder simply becomes fed up? These are legitimate concerns, not only for the NCCPG committee, but also for those responsible at county level. It was a problem of that sort of order that faced Pat and her Dorset colleagues when the salvia collection was suddenly affected by change.

The reason for having a National Collection of *Salvia* was not really to preserve the annual

***Salvia sclarea* var *turkestanica:* study of the flowerhead.**
Photo Philip Vlasto.

Salvia urica:
flowerhead study.
Photo Philip Vlasto.

salvias that are set out in ranks like little scarlet soldiers in park bedding schemes, but to collect together the extremely wide range of perennial species so that they could be studied properly. There was and is to date no monograph on *Salvia*, there was considerable confusion surrounding them, and nobody had previously gathered them together for accurate comparison. It is hardly recognised at all that there are some great beauties among salvias. They are rarely seen in gardens, partly because many species will not stand the winter unless in an exceptionally mild part of the country. They are relatively short-lived, too, but are easily kept going by over-wintered cuttings.

There are few cultivars among them apart from the well-known forms of the hardy species and hybrids, such as *S. x superba* , forms of which – 'May Night', 'East Friesland', 'Lubeca', and so on – are easily found in garden centres. The culinary sage, *S. officinalis* and its variants,

are, of course, to be found in every herb patch. One or two, however, such as the 'Cambridge Blue' form of *S. patens*, need insurance against their eventually disappearing from lists. On the whole, though, this is a genus whose species, as opposed to forms raised in gardens, need to be preserved in cultivation.

Pat's contact with the head gardener of a large garden near the coast resulted in the collection finding a home. The garden was open to the public, and a particularly successful year allowed the building of a greenhouse specifically intended to house the more tender salvias. Salvias loathe growing in pots, showing their disapproval by refusing to grow properly, while making so many long, questing roots that no pots can contain them. They have to be allowed free rein in beds or they will sulk themselves to death.

In an open-air plot devoted to them, *Salvia concolor* annually renewed its stout stems that towered 2.4m (8ft) or more over its large, heart-shaped leaves and produced showers of pure blue flowers that sometimes lasted until Christmas. The brilliant crimson *S. grahamii*, more shrubby but half as tall, was the subject of much speculation about its 'correct' name. The whole area was alive with blues, purples, scarlets and even yellow, while in the greenhouse, salvias that hardly anyone had seen before found a safe haven.

Philip brought his scientific mind to bear, and he applied a lifetime's research know-how to the collection, assembling nine books of records, photographs, measurements, and just about everything that had been authoritatively written about salvia species. That his material does not constitute a monograph is only because it has not been cast in monograph form. He is an authority on the genus *Salvia*, although he refuses to admit it.

This happy state of affairs was not to last. The head gardener was not his own boss and was subject to the policies of a country estate management newly converted to commercial-mindedness and freshly acquainted with the profit motive. The salvias were deemed to be uninteresting to the average paying visitor to the garden, and the greenhouse was to be made more exciting by clearing out the salvias and putting on a show of tropical exotica. Without adequate housing, a collection of plants that were by no means all hardy could no longer be maintained.

Not long afterwards the head gardener (who

was a gardener simply because he had turned his back on a life in commerce many years previously) left. Pat and Philip, whose part in keeping the collection going had greatly increased, determined that it should be moved in its entirety. The question was, where?

They had already moved to Child Okeford and were looking forward to making a new garden there and enjoying a proper retirement. They did not feel that they could take on a collection of the size of *Salvia*, and besides, it would take resources greater than private individuals could reasonably be asked to provide.

The solution arrived as a direct result of the sorts of relationships that people with a close interest in plants and gardens always seem to enjoy. The Dorset College of Agriculture and Horticulture had for several years provided the venues for the Dorset NCCPG group's meetings and, moreover, the horticultural staff had played a highly positive part in its activities, including holding the National Collection of *Penstemons*.

In South Wales, Dyffryn Botanical Gardens, under the management of Stephen Torode, had a long-standing and quite comprehensive collection of salvias that had been put together independently. The Vlastos had been in touch several times, comparing notes and exchanging plant material, so that Dyffryn seemed ideally suited to taking over the collection with the exception of the tender species that the college would now look after.

Pat and Philip settled down to keeping a sort of parental watching brief over the collection, sometimes coming across new material, which they handed over to the care of people whom they knew would run the collection as it should be run. The plants seemed safe from having their fate decided by others whose decisions (or whims) would be most unlikely to be influenced by such things as the well-being of plants.

Once again, however, misfortune overtook the collection. The college never faltered in its dedication to this fascinating genus of plants, but events at Dyffryn almost uncannily followed the pattern of the previous home of the collection, and a large part of it was once more to be on the move.

The story of the salvia collection – continued, but not concluded in the next chapter – is not one that should cause apprehension; rather we should be glad to know that conservation of garden plants has become such a deep-seated concern that it transcends the comings and

goings that attend modern life. It also lends strength to Anne Stevens' belief that the larger collections should be split if possible. Each part is then in a position to absorb the stock of another should it become necessary.

The way in which the collection has been managed is a fine example to all gardeners, let alone those with a national responsibility. Good gardeners keep good records, but Philip's are an outstanding instance of organisation applied to horticulture and an embodiment of what the founders of the NCCPG might have had in mind had they imagined that the idea of National Collections would have engendered the sort of long-term, intelligent enthusiasm that it has.

The collection is a source of knowledge and plant material from a genus that has hitherto been almost unknown to gardeners. We now know that there is a very large group of plants, far more bright and showy – even exotic – than we might have supposed, which can provide our gardens with colour and elegance of form for months on end.

If we have to take a few cuttings each year as insurance against winter cold, it seems a small price to pay.

***Salvia oppositifolia:* scale study for the National Collection record.**
Photo Philip Vlasto.

Dyffryn: **Collections in Trouble**

The very fact that National Collections of plants are in the care of people – ordinary human beings – means that there is always an element of risk attached to their existence. Certainly their permanence is not something that can be taken for granted.

Not much more than two years after the *Salvia* collection was reorganised, disaster struck part of it. We saw in the previous chapter how it moved in part to the Dorset College of Agriculture and Horticulture, and in part to Dyffryn, near Cardiff, where it absorbed the existing informal collection. Dyffryn now shared in two collections; *Salvia* and *Dahlia*.

The story of Dyffryn is as fascinating as it is undoubtedly sad. It is situated in the Vale of Glamorgan, seven miles west of the centre of Cardiff, close to the charming village of St Nicholas. The site was the home of the Bishops of Llandaff for almost 900 years until bought by

A Small Decorative dahlia at Dyffryn, unlabelled.
Photo John Kelly.

the Button family in the 16th century. Thomas Button, a contemporary of Raleigh and Rear Admiral under Hawkins, knew the estate as Worlton, and it became known as Dyffryn St Nicholas only in the 18th century.

It was the Cory family who rebuilt Dyffryn at the end of the 19th century. They made their money from South Wales coal and turned their profit into a mansion on a scale to rival the grandest Loire châteaux. The house has two 'fronts' in different styles, the more Palladian of which stares haughtily down the length of an enormous panorama of lawns and terraces, the heart of an astonishing 55 acres of gardens.

The river that wound through the grounds was tamed, canalised, and forced underground. Beyond its conduit lies a semi-circle of trees, known for many years to the gardeners as the 'arbour'. Only recently has it emerged that the stream had been designed to reappear in order to provide boating for the Cory family. The trees ringed not an arbour, but the 'harbour' for the boats.

Reginald Cory was a distinguished amateur of horticulture who held the offices of Vice President of the Royal Horticultural Society and President of the National Dahlia Society. Between 1906 and 1915 he supervised the design of the present garden by Thomas Mawson, of whose work it is probably the best, if not the only complete example. Cory's introductions from abroad were important, varied, and brilliantly planted. He interested himself in trees and shrubs from the Orient, as well as succulents and, of course, dahlias. As a result, the gardens contain superb examples of such treasures as *Magnolia macrophylla* – hardly ever seen as a free-standing specimen – the paper bark maple (*Acer griseum*) raised from the original seed from the collector, E.H. Wilson, the rare Chinese wingnut (*Pterocarya stenocarpa*), and the Japanese oak, *Quercus aliena*. In the glasshouses are bananas, avocados, cinnamon, orange, grapefruit, cacti, succulents, and a host of other exotics. There is an Italian garden, a garden devoted entirely to fuchsias, and even a Roman (Pompeian) garden, perfect in every detail or almost so.

Over the whole there reigns an atmosphere of decay – genteel decay to be sure, but with a certainty about it akin to that which surrounded the Irish Ascendancy earlier in the present century. The clothes are of high quality and superb cut, but the fabric is threadbare, although expertly and almost invisibly mended.

It is not easy for the modern mind to recon-

An unlabelled Ball dahlia at Dyffryn - could it be 'Opal'?
Photo John Kelly.

cile the conditions under which Welsh miners worked and lived with the sumptuous leisure enjoyed by the Cory family. If the huge lawn, quite large enough for a first-class cricket match, seemed not quite to match the level of the edge of the central canal, the order was given to raise it by six inches – and it was done forthwith with no thought to cost. Such estates as these provided considerable employment, it is true, but the gulf between the most benevolent owner of such a palace and those who provided his comfort seems now to have been unconscionably wide.

It all had to end, of course. Such grandiose dwellings can no longer be sustained in private hands and those that still hang on tenuously find the years successively clarifying the fate that must await them. Change of use may put off their demise, tourism may provide a stay of execution of some years, but a house and garden such as Dyffryn, built on a scale that can never be justified again, has no escape from ultimate oblivion.

Thus it is that Mid Glamorgan County Council find it worthwhile to run the house as an efficient conference centre. For several years they supported the gardens and its diverse and

Dyffryn: unlabelled dahlia. With groups of plants containing so many varieties, accurate labelling is vital. There is no place for guesswork.
Photo John Kelly.

important collections of plants. But it has to be said that the gardens are impressive only in parts and the best that can realistically be achieved is to keep them tidy. One feels glad that the much reduced garden staff can feel optimistic about renovation of the enormous greenhouses and the Italian garden, but sad too, because one can see beyond the bowed structures and slipped panes the shaken heads

of unconvinced accountants.

Policies – perhaps unavoidable, possibly just sensible – failed to find echoes in the heart of the senior horticultural figure. Perhaps it was a mistake to allow the place to be called Dyffryn Botanical Gardens... Whatever the reason, it is evident that the aspirations of a dedicated professional gardener and the restraints imposed by inevitable decline were irreconcil-

Previous page: **The terrace below the windows of the house at Dyffryn (used as a conference centre).** Photo John Kelly.

Dyffryn: Dahlia 'Bishop of Llandaff'. Photo John Kelly.

able. Once more, the salvia collection was to fall victim to perceptions of economic reality, in which the Head Gardener, along with the Head Gamekeeper, deserve places in the red data book of human occupations.

The *Salvia* and *Dahlia* collections at Dyffryn have been suspended. It is particularly tragic in the case of the dahlias, so beloved of Reginald Cory, as Glamorgan has a place in the history of dahlias that should never be allowed to die.

In front of the house now is set annually a long bed of the wickedly red, single-flowered dahlia 'Bishop of Llandaff'. It was one of several sent from Dyffryn to the then bishop along with a request that he should choose one to be named after his Office. That he could not resist the bronze-leaved beauty, even though its red belongs more to Beelzebub than episcopacy, is not surprising; it is one of the most celebrated flowers of all time.

This gorgeous dahlia was not nearly as well known a few years ago as it is now. Its present popularity can be credited to the NCCPG, under whose aegis it was vigorously propagated and distributed. It is one of the few dahlia cultivars that appear to be long-lived and there seems no reason why we should not enjoy its satanic loveliness for many more decades.

It is profoundly to be hoped that success attends the enterprises at Dyffryn. However, whether it does or not, the fact remains that the place gave us one of the most influential plantsmen of the 20th century, whose award, the Reginal Cory Cup, is given for new hybrid plants.

Neither should it be forgotten that one such hybrid, a roguish dahlia, may serve to remind us of that long 900 years when the Bishops of Llandaff saw no reason to doubt the permanence of their tenure.

Paul Picton:
Michaelmas Daisies

The Christian festival of Michaelmas is not just the feast day of St Michael. It is also the day when tradition has it that all harvests should be in and the land ready for the winter, whose chills begin to be felt as the leaves colour russet and gold before they fall. It is a quarterly rent day in England; you could not expect a man to quit his land before he had gained all he could from it, nor make a present of apples or late grain to the new tenant.

Apples grow well in the county that used to be Worcestershire before soulless men decreed that it should become part of Hereford and Worcester. There are fruit for eating and cooking of course, but this is also the northernmost arm of the west country cider belt, where rolling accents, rolling roads and a certain late evening gait are not uncommon.

The steep thrust of the Malvern Hills out of the gently undulating plain is unexpected, sudden, and quite un-English. It is almost as if their sharp, commanding ridge were a sentry for the mountains of Wales. Great Malvern, a colony of interconnected villages, looks from

Top left: **Aster novi-belgii 'Cloudy Blue'.**

Top right: **Aster novi-belgii 'Anita Ballard'.**

Below left: **Aster novi-belgii 'Marie Ballard'.**

Below right: **Aster amellus 'Sternkugel'.**

All photos John Kelly.

its sunny slopes across the Midlands, while on the other, steeper side, tucked at the bottom of a winding road that the Roman miners used, is the village of Colwall.

Not many people have heard of Colwall, but in gardening terms it is more important than many a large town. It has a horticultural society with more than 200 members, which administers a Memorial Fund that finances not only an annual lecture but a prize for the best student at Pershore College of Horticulture – and has within its purlieu the National Collection of Michaelmas Daisies.

If you visit the Picton Garden in late September, you are likely to find the collection approaching its best. It varies a little from year to year, of course, but the flowers in general respect their eponymous season and appear on cue. As so often is the case, the collection is in commercial hands, and the garden is attached to a nursery, but it would be an insensitive soul indeed who felt able to bracket Picton's with the general run of nurseries, let alone with what we understand by commerce.

It is not that Paul and Meriel Picton are unprofessional. On the contrary, they are pro-

Aster novae-angliae **'Rosa Seiger'**.
Photo John Kelly.

Varieties of Novi-Belgii asters in the Picton Garden, 19th September. Photo John Kelly.

fessional enough to be able to be just about as commercial or non-commercial as they wish to be. The tall, quietly spoken Paul and his vivacious wife, Meriel, work very hard and bring to the running of Old Court Nursery a vivid intelligence that allows them to run their business without letting it run them. It leaves them time, as the saying goes, to smell the flowers.

Paul's father Percy was born in 1904 at Great Missenden, Buckinghamshire, the son of a gamekeeper. His mother made him take up gardening and he was apprenticed at 'Boswells', near Wendover, the home of Sir Thomas Barlow. Later he went to work for William Robinson of Gravetye Manor, one of the great figures of gardening in the early part of the century, who was designer, plantsman, writer and controversialist. There he met such near-legendary figures as the great plantswoman, Miss Ellen Willmott (who lived at Warley Hall in Essex and had forty gardeners in her vegetable garden alone) and worked under Ernest Markham, of clematis fame.

When he rose to become head gardener to Miss Hopton, at Hagley Court, near Hereford, he raised classic clematis hybrids such as 'Hagley Hybrid', but it was in 1948, when Ernest Ballard asked him to manage his Michaelmas daisy nursery at Colwall, that Percy's feet were set on the plant-breeding trail that was to bring him fame.

He bought the business on Ballard's death and from then on never allowed commercial considerations to interfere with helping others to know and love plants. He travelled the country lecturing on shrubs, alpine and herbaceous plants and as a show judge, and in his later years shone as a true 'natural' on television gardening programmes.

I met Percy Picton once or twice almost a quarter of a century ago and found him captivating. In his soft country accent he could tease, disagree, correct and instruct, while the michievous twinkle in his eye never dimmed for a second. To any slightly pompous statement he was likely to feign astonishment: 'Well, now. I didn't know that!' He died in 1985 and it is the Percy Picton Memorial Fund Appeal into which the Wyche and Colwall Horticultural Society understandably put so much of their energy.

***Aster novi-belgii*
'Crimson Bro-
cade'.**
Photo John Kelly.

The Michaelmas Daisy (*Aster*) Collection is planted in semi-cottage style in the Picton Garden. It is kept in the proper tradition of a National Collection, with many of the varieties having no commercial application nowadays. As a place to study asters it is perfect. You can spend hours comparing varieties, getting to know colours, heights and habits, and learning much about how best to deploy them in the garden.

The three main kinds are *Aster novi-belgii* (New York Asters), *A. novae-angliae* (New England) and the forms of *Aster amellus*, the Italian starwort. Apart from these, *Aster x frikartii* – a small group of excellent hybrids – and some small-flowered species make up the bulk of what are collectively called Michaelmas daisies.

It is, in fact, incorrect to write of *Novi-belgii* and *Novae Angliae* asters as if they were species. *A. novi-belgii* itself has been hybridised with others and a wide range of cultivars

developed over nearly 300 years. You may occasionally see mauve asters growing beside the railway line, and these approach the original introductions. *A. novae-angliae* is reluctant to hybridise, and although its characteristics are not that far removed from plants in the wild in North America, it is highly unlikely that there is no other species represented in their make-up.

The plant breeders have had most of their fun with the *Novi-belgii* asters because of their propensity for producing new forms. They are plants for sunny positions but greatly love a moisture-retentive soil. Their worst attribute, however, is a martyrdom to mildew.

To keep them looking good, they must be regularly sprayed with a modern systemic fungicide and most, especially the more modern, taller varieties, which are anything from 90cm (3ft) to 1.5m (5ft) high, need to be securely staked. The weight of the flowers is such that they topple easily, especially after rain.

Nevertheless, they are rightly extremely popular, because the autumn garden is the poorer without them and some of the colours are quite ravishing. There are whites, such as 'Blandie', which is 90cm (3ft) high; pale pinks like the double 'Fellowship', 1.05m (3.5ft), and dark pinks, among which 'Brightest and Best', a fine, 90cm (3ft), large double thoroughly deserves its name. Reds like 'Helen Ballard' leaven the preponderance of lavender-blues and purples, which culminate in the 1.2m (4ft), deep violet-blue 'Harrison's Blue'. The range of colours is also to be found in varieties of medium height – 60cm (2ft) and less – and in dwarf cultivars – Michaelmas daisies only 30cm (1ft) high – that are suitable for the smallest gardens

If you ask for the 90cm (3ft) 'Cloudy Blue' before March, when propagating is done, a plant or plants will be kept for you, but you will not find it on the commercial list. It is looked after with great care in the collection, however, as it is of great interest historically. It was raised in 1914 and at the time was a break in aster colour. It is one of the most apt and beautiful names ever given to a plant, and describes perfectly the colour of the slightly irregular, partially double flowers.

Thirty years onward, 'Anita Ballard' made its appearance, with the colour deepened and the tendency towards doubling considerably enhanced. It was recognised even then as only a step along the road that might lead to the perfect, double, blue *Novi-belgii* aster. After another thirty years, Picton's 'Marie Ballard' arrived. It is a notable improvement on 'Anita Ballard', but still does not match up to the aspirations of the Picton family. One day another significant step will be taken, but until then this fascinating trio can be seen in the Picton garden where they are grown, not as part of a shop-window dressing, but as a living demonstration of the plant breeder's art and ultra-long-term vision. A collection like this shows that those who are truly dedicated to the breeding of plants are quite capable of seeing their own lifetimes as mere episodes.

You might not think, having seen that *Novae Angliae* asters breed reluctantly, that advances were easy to come by, and you would be right. While there are over 300 varieties of *Novi-belgii* asters on the market generally, there are just a little less than one tenth their number of *Novae-Angliae* varieties. (While speaking of statistics, Pictons' commercial list of *Novi-belgii* asters, one of the most comprehensive in the country,

represents only 40 per cent of the varieties growing in the National Collection.)

Nevertheless, improvements do come along. It might well have been thought that 'Harrington's Pink', a clear rose-pink with no blue tint, was unlikely to be improved upon, yet 'Rosa Seiger', 30cm (1ft) shorter and of the most pure rose-pink, is decidedly better. It is often the fate of improved-upon plants such as 'Harrington's Pink' to disappear from cultivation altogether, but then how would we know in its case just how much better 'Rosa Seiger' is? If superseded plants are kept going in National Collections, the standard of those that supplanted them can be measured, as can the chances of making further improvements.

Aster amellus is an Italian species, short, tough and, like *Novae Angliae* asters, resistant to mildew. For some reason its varieties are not much in demand. Maybe it is because they are not thought of as 'Michaelmas daisies', and indeed they do flower a little earlier, but you will find the lovely, lavender-blue 'Sternkugel' hiding its foliage under large blooms precisely at Michaelmas at Picton's. Visit a truly representative National Collection and your perspectives will surely be widened.

The Picton Garden is no dusty museum of plants. It is a celebration of the genus *Aster*, certainly, but it is also a demonstration of the plant associations in which they are at their most felicitous. Would you, for example, have thought of interplanting your roses with the shorter-growing asters? In the rose garden at the bottom of the Picton Garden the late blooms of pink, white and the softer red roses tone beautifully with the simpler, shorter asters.

In another part of the garden the bold, richly golden, dark-eyed daisies of *Rudbeckia* 'Goldsturm' make a dramatic punctuation mark among the pinks, reds, lilacs and purples of the asters, and the perfection with which asters blend with *Schizostylis coccinea* and sedums of the *S. spectabile* persuasion has to be seen to be appreciated.

So many gardens are over by the time the September equinox arrives. It is a terrible shame and similar to watching two acts of a fine play, only to have the final curtain come down with the third act omitted entirely. This superb National Collection fulfils every criterion laid down by the NCCPG and then goes much further. It demonstrates an entire dimension of gardening about whose existence so many of us know very little.

Terence Read: Citrus, Figs and Greenhouse Grapes

Hales Hall, in the heart of Norfolk, is the site of one of the most unusual nurseries in the country. Discreet signs lead you down a little lane, across a cattle grid, and on to a gravel track through a wide field in which dozy cows and calves condescend eventually to get out of your way. Cross a second grid and you find yourself in another century.

Ancient buildings enclose a broad quadrangle of lawns, flower beds, young topiary and straight, gravel paths. On one side is a gatehouse in warm old brick between weatherbeaten timbers, converted by Terence and Judy Read along with the adjacent Steward's House into a home in which modern influences mix happily with early Tudor. James Hobart, Attorney General to Henry VII for 21 years, lived in the great house of which this was once the courtyard, and his huge barn, quite as large as many monastic tithe barns of his time, occupies one entire side and now constitutes what is probably Britain's oldest garden shed.

Behind it is a thoroughly modern nursery. It is renowned among plantspeople for what might loosely be called conservatory plants. If you want an oleander, there are more than a dozen to choose from. Unusual passion flowers, daturas, abutilons and an unrivalled selec-

'Osborne's Prolific', a very productive fig with a rich, sweet flavour.
Photo Reads Nursery.

Fig 'Rouge de Bordeaux' at the perfect stage of ripeness.
Photo Reads Nursery.

tion of twenty-odd varieties of bougainvillea wait to be carried off gleefully or depatched carefully by post to conservatories and greenhouses everywhere.

The catalogue announces that Reads have been nurserymen since 1890, but in fact they have been growing plants commercially for much longer; that is merely the year from which the current enterprise can be said to date. Terence and Judy have been at Hales Hall for twenty years – a mere moment in the family's horticultural history.

You might think, on hearing that Terence looks after no fewer than three national collections, that they would be run on the same commercial lines as the rest of the nursery stock. You would be partially right, but would probably be surprised to find him working very hard on occasion to talk people out of buying certain varieties. It is easy to be cynical about the nursery trade, but no nurseryman will willingly sell a plant to a customer who will find it too difficult, and all the good ones try their best to suit the plant to the customer. After all, it not only keeps the clientele happy, but also ensures that they will come back again.

Terence Read takes particular care with citrus, figs and greenhouse grapes because some of them are profoundly difficult unless you have the expertise that comes with talent married to many years of experience. Whereas many groups of plants – including ferociously tricky alpines – are perfectly within the competence of amateur gardeners, many tropical and sub-tropical fruits need the constant attention that only a professional is equipped to give when more than just a few are grown together.

Sometimes it is the most temperamental and demanding that are the ones most deserving of being kept in good condition, as they have a way of being genetically significant. One of the main thrusts of maintaining a national collection of fruit is to conserve the genetic stock that is the basis of present and future varieties. If a variety is lost it may never be re-created, but as long as its parents are alive there is a possibility of coming close.

The fig collection is perhaps the most astonishing of the three. Most gardeners know 'Brown Turkey', and that is about all, but Reads have upwards of twenty figs in their catalogue at any one time. You can choose from varieties that are good on walls out of doors, more suited to pots, or equally happy under both regimes. There are figs with red, yellow, pink or white flesh, yellow, black, purple, pink or brown skin, and even one (Panachée), whose green and yellow stripes put one in mind of a flight of hot-air balloons.

Figs have been grown in Britain since Roman times but originated in the Persian Empire and are not uniformly hardy. It is unlikely that

that are no longer grown for commercial figs are still excellent garden plants, and it would be a great shame if they were lost. The National Collection of Figs has in common with that of old-fashioned shrub roses at Mottisfont Abbey, Hampshire, the aim of preserving history in botanical form.

The names of the varieties, many of which have several synonyms, are redolent of their long establishment in cultivation. 'White Marseilles', for example, has in its time been known as White Naples, Figue Blanche, White Standard, White Genoa and Raby Castle. 'Violette Dauphine', a violet-skinned fig with strawberry flesh, was also named Grosse Violette and Rouge d'Argenteuil. The amount of research Terence has had to do in order to determine which of the names for 'Brunswick' is currently valid – others are Clementine, Brown Hamburg, Bayswater and White Turkey – is impressive, and there are many other jungles of synonyms into which he has had to plunge.

Of a list of 26 recommended figs given in *Thompson's Garden Assistant* at the turn of the last century, when Reads Nurseries had been established for just a decade, 'Angélique', 'Black

descendants of those very early introductions still exist, but you can buy 'White Marseilles' from Reads Nurseries in the knowledge that trees of it planted by Cardinal Pole at Lambeth Palace in 1525 are still flourishing. Built in 1480, Hales Hall was almost new then.

Fig varieties are often old, but retain their garden-worthiness for a very long time. Many

Far left: **Fig 'Violette Sepor' is a heavy cropper when grown in pots in the greenhouse.** Photo Reads Nursery.

Left: **Reads Nursery produced this record, prize-winning bunch of the early muscat grape 'Madresfield Court' in 1905.**

Ischia', 'Brown Turkey', 'Brunswick', 'Bourjassotte Grise' (then also known as 'Grizzly Bourjassotte'), 'Castle Kennedy', 'Negro Largo', 'Panachée', 'Rouge de Bordeaux', 'St Johns', 'White Ischia' and 'White Marseilles' are still propagated and sold by them.

Figs can be prolific in their growth and can make very large specimens, especially when fan-trained on warm walls. However, in order to bear fruit in good quantity without there ensuing a wait of several years, they must be restricted at the root. The hardiest figs are only possible out of doors in the warmer parts of the country, and a comprehensive collection is only possible under glass.

This applies to citrus, too. They are also long lived plants, the life spans of specimens in the gardens of some Italian villas being measured in centuries. However, unlike figs, citrus have seen great advances in the present century, especially in Florida and California, where enormous citrus groves stretch to the horizon.

The National Collection represents the varieties that can be grown in Britain either entirely under glass or which may be brought out of doors during the summer months. They have, therefore, to be amenable to pot culture. It includes, however, the sweet orange 'Valencia Late', which was the foundation variety of the Californian citrus industry.

Florida and California have distinct climates, the one sub-tropical with a dry winter and wet summer, the other mediterranean, with winter rainfall and a dry summer. Citrus varieties do not necessarily do well in both. 'Valencia Late' is not only the best sweet orange for California; it is also the most widely grown orange in the world. It was discovered growing in Madeira in the 1850s and named 'Excelsior' by the firm of Rivers of Sawbridgeworth, who introduced it to Britain and exported it to California, thus founding that State's citrus industry. The Americans renamed it 'Valencia Late', although it had never set its roots on Spanish soil. Rivers also introduced foundation citrus varieties into Florida.

Rivers closed down in 1983 after 250 years in the nursery business, the family having dispersed all over the world. Reads, who had always grown a few citrus, and who were close colleagues of Rivers, bought their entire stock, and added it to their own to form the basis of what is now the national collection. This was something of a close call, as the necessity for conserving cultivars had not yet been fully realised and nobody else wanted them. Among them were some great treasures, such as a thornless Seville orange – heaven sent when the average Seville is, in Terence's words, 'armed like a fortress'.

Among the Reads' varieties of citrus are sweet and bitter oranges, mandarins (including satsumas), lemons, limes, grapefruit, kumquat, limequat, citron, shaddock, tangelo, tangor and calamondin. Many of them, raised in the United States, have found their way back to where they can stand in the same glasshouse as those old varieties that gave them their start.

The greenhouse grapes collection is as impressive as the figs. Again, taking the list of pre-1900 varieties in *Thompson's Garden Assistant*, of 27 that appear there, Reads' 1992 catalogue listed 17, as well at least a dozen others, current in the 19th century, that do not appear in *Thompson*.

Greenhouse grapes are increasingly popular as the vogue for conservatories grows. They are not difficult to cultivate and can be grown and fruited as standards in containers. They are usually kept to about 1.2m (4ft) high and have their lateral growths stopped at two leaves past each bunch of grapes. In mid to late December, the laterals are pruned hard back to two buds.

There are three principal kinds; sweetwater grapes, muscats, and vinous. Sweetwater grapes are, as you might imagine, sweetly juicy. They have thin skins and do not keep well but are the first to ripen. They are the best ones to grow in completely unheated glass structures. 'Black Prince' and 'King's Ruby' are black sweetwaters; 'Buckland Sweetwater' and 'Madeleine 'Royale' are white.

Muscats are the next to ripen but need a little heat to mature, and a minimum temperature of 7°C (45°F) between ripening and picking is essential. It is worth bearing in mind that during the ripening season, frosts readily occur. However, once the grapes are harvested, no heat is required during the winter. Winter heat is, in general, detrimental to vines, which need a period of dormancy. The roots of container-grown vines are, however, frost-tender. 'Black Frontignan' and 'Angers Frontignan' (both black) and 'Auvergne Frontignan' and 'Royal Muscadine' (both white) are examples of easily grown muscats.

Vinous grapes ripen last and have excellent keeping qualities, although they need a longer period of heat for ripening. Although you might

Part of the extensive glasshouses that house the National Collections at Reads.
Photo John Kelly.

Above, far left:
Citrus 'Meyer's Lemon'.

Above left: **'Meyer's Lemon' in flower and fruit.**

Far left: **Mandarin 'Ortanique'.**

Left: **Orange 'Valencia Late', the foundation of the American citrus industry.**

Photos Reads Nursery.

suppose the well known 'Black Hamburgh' to be a vinous grape it is, in fact, a sweetwater. Among black vinous grapes are 'Gros Colmar', 'Gros Maroc' and 'West's St Peters'; white ones include 'Golden Queen' and 'Trebbiano'.

The costs involved in housing, heating and maintaining meaningful national collections of these three groups of fruit mean that they really have to be in professional hands. The collection of outdoor grapes, including both those grown for dessert and for wine, is also cared for by professionals, split between experts on fruit and wine grapes. Reads' selection of about thirty is by no means to be forgotten as a repository of these plants, but one feels that Terence and Judy and their son Stephen are making a more than adequate contribution to the conservation of cultivated plants as it is.

Orange 'Washington Navel'.
Photo Reads Nursery.

Jenny Burgess: **Sisyrinchium**

To be a National Collection holder involves much more than simply collecting together a group of plants and keeping them going. Botanical science advances at an accelerating rate as new techniques lead to fresh understanding. Indeed, it is far from unlikely that before long we shall find ourselves witnessing the world's entire flora being put through a complete revision of its classification.

Gardeners are healthily resistant to change, so much so that cases have been known of durable labels being correct twice in their lifetimes. An example is the mat-forming, lime-hating, sun-loving alpine *Lithodora diffusa*, usually grown as the cultivar 'Heavenly Blue' or the similar 'Grace Ward'. In Gertrude Jekyll's day it was *Lithodora diffusa*, but was then reclassified under the name many of us have come to know well; *Lithospermum diffusum*. Recently, however, when botanical opinion once again swung behind the earlier name, the wheel had turned full circle.

Strictly speaking, there is no such thing as a 'correct' botanical name. Names are accepted or rejected according to the weight of authoritative opinion. For example, a rare Rocky Mountain alpine, confined to Pike's Peak in Colorado, had been known since its discovery as *Boykinia jamesii* in honour of Dr Boykin, botanist, of the State of Georgia. During the 1970s, American botanists, dissatisfied with its classification on the reasonable grounds that it had twice the number of stamens as any other boykinia species, coined for it the new genus *Telesonix*. That it reads more like a patented method of producing video sound is neither here nor there.

Agreement or otherwise has nothing to do with euphonics. *Telesonix jamesii* became accepted as a taxon because the bulk of authoritative botanical opinion gathered behind it. You don't have to like the name, but if you want to be as accurate as possible – and in the final analysis if you wish to communicate about

Sisyrinchium bellum, now reclassified as *S. idahoense*.
Photo John Kelly.

Sisyrinchium **'Quaint and Queer'.**
Photo John Kelly.

plants – you do have to accept it.

Jenny Burgess, who holds the National Collection of *Sisyrynchium* near Loddon, in the Norfolk Broads, is faced with an immediate reevaluation of the genus. Her house is in a tiny hamlet, hidden away in a fold of the deep countryside and reached only by means of narrow lanes that twist and turn with a thoroughly satisfactory lack of logic. She lives in the boondocks, but has her finger firmly on the pulse of botanical opinion, which is just as well, as the botanists have descended on sisyrinchiums like a Revenue raid.

They are small plants in the main, mostly 20cm (8in) tall, and ideal for the rock garden, scree or raised bed, where they flower in summer. At first sight they are very similar to the smaller bulbous irises, but their flowers are symmetrical and star-shaped, looking up at you happily when the sun shines, but folding up in

dull weather. The genus is confined to the Americas, apart from one species, which somehow island-hopped via Bermuda to the west of Ireland.

A taller, border species, *Sisyrinchium striatum*, has been whisked away into a new genus as *Phaiophleps nigricans.* Such complete changes are not easy to cope with, as all clues are gone when you come to consult an older book or article and wish to read further in a modern work. To give another example, how many of us, reading Gertrude Jekyll, would know where to find out more about the plant she knew as *Agathaea coelestis?* A trained researcher with access to a large enough botanical library will, after some effort, discover that it is now *Felicia amelloides,* but what about the rest of us?

Jenny must also wonder what on earth botanists are up to when they take no notice

Sisyrinchium striatum, which botanical opinion considers to be **Phaiophleps nigricans.**
Photo Nicola Kelly.

Part of Jenny Burgess' National Collection of *Sisyrinchium* - small plants, large nomenclature problem.
Photo John Kelly.

whatever of differences between plants which, to a gardener, seem to make the lumping together of genera quite at variance with appearances.

One must answer such common sense observations by pointing out that the variation within a species can be very wide, so that specimens taken from opposite ends of the spectrum of wild plants may very well look different enough to seem to be distinct species. Botanists, who see the larger picture, know the true state of affairs.

Sisyrinchium bellum, violet-blue, veined with purple, and with a yellow throat, has always been a favourite of alpine gardeners. It flowers over a long season, from June to August, and is a neat, floriferous, sun-loving plant about 20cm (8in) high. *S. macounii*, as we have known it, is half the height and has large, purple flowers. Its delightful white form was at one time thought to be the 'type' of the species. Another

white sisyrinchium, early flowering and known as 'May Snow', is similar.

Jenny suddenly has to get used to lumping this group of plants into one genus – *S. idahoense*. The white form of *S. macounii* and 'May Snow' are regarded as the same and are now *S. idahoense album*. *S. bellum* disappears, to be subsumed into *S. idahoense*.

All this would on the face of it make more sense if *S. angustifolium*, 15cm (6in) tall and similar to *S. bellum*, were included in *S. idahoense*. Not so, however. It not only remains as a species in its own right but in its turn swallows up the well-known, now ex-species, *S. bermudianum*, the sisyrinchium that invaded Ireland.

Nevertheless, if science is to progress, and of course it must, gardeners will have to grit their teeth and bear it. Botanists cannot be expected to take gardeners into consideration when rearranging the names of plants according to the information before them. It would make life easier, however, if they could possibly do so when coining new ones.

Botany has over-ruled those of us who would issue dire warnings against the yellow-flowered *S. brachypus*, whose powers of colonisation make the 19th century British look like amateurs. Its seedlings have a way of issuing from the middle of choice cushion plants or riveting themselves into cracks in rock from which there is no prospect of removing them. It is now part of *S. californicum*, referred to as *S. californicum* Brachypus Group, whatever that means. The old *S. brachypus* was a plant always of less than 15cm (6in), whereas *S. californicum*, as we have known it, was from 20cm (8in) to 30cm (1ft) in height. It was also, although capable of seeding itself, nothing like as territorially ambitious as *S. brachypus*.

All this is hardly good bedtime reading, but Jenny Burgess, deep in her Norfolk fastness, must keep up with it if her tenure of the National Collection is to be carried out to the standard she and the NCCPG require. She is of the opinion that it would be nice if 'they' would inform collection holders of changes of nomenclature, and she has a point. In July, 1992, a large plant of *Sisyrinchium striatum* at the Royal Horticultural Society's garden at Wisley had, in front of its old, black, engraved label, a temporary, hand-written, white one that informed passers-by of its transfer to the genus *Phaiophleps*. If there is an appropriate time for leading horticultural institutions to change a label, it is also the right moment for a National Collection holder to change hers, but who is to inform her of the new name? Would it not be a good idea for the NCCPG to collate nomenclatural changes into an annual information sheet for holders of National Collections?

Jenny is a quiet woman, but her views on certain matters are quite decided. About the NCCPG she declares that it is 'about time someone came up with some sponsorship', and about *Syrinchiums* she admits that the seeding habits of the ex- *S. brachypus* have given the genus a bad name. 'You either love them or hate them, but more and more people are coming to love them as I do'.

It is easy to share her enthusiasm, especially for two species that are entirely different from the others. *S. douglasii*, a plant that disappears completely after flowering, has drooping bells of wine-purple in July and August on 20cm (8in) stems. *S. filifolium*, from the Falklands, is similar, but its flowers are white and veined with purple.

How long will it be, one wonders, before these two are hived off into some new genus all of their own? Will the botanists try to find a name that is at once appropriate and pleasant to say and hear? Will the obscurity that renaming leads to result in the loss of two lovely plants from our garden flora?

Not, one feels, if Jenny Burgess has anything to do with it. Because, even if they were to be removed from the remit of the holder of the sisyrinchium collection, there is nothing bureaucratic about her love of good plants, whatever their names may be.

Below:
Sisyrinchium macounii album, now also reclassified as a form of **S. idahoense.**

Bottom:
Sisyrinchium 'Sisland Blue'.
Photos John Kelly.

Ann and Roger Bowden:
Hosta

Hostas are cool, leafy plants, capable of being grown in just about any garden, and virtually essential in most. They readily make large, verdant clumps and can be relied on to push their sharp noses through the soil every spring, ready to unfurl their unmistakable, heart-shaped leaves in shades of green, grey and blue.

They flower, too, with lily-like blooms from lilac-purple to white, and the recent description of them as the flowering foliage plants is certainly apt. Some are fragrant, and a few modern hybrids are almost good enough when in flower to make you forget for a moment that they are primarily grown for their leafiness.

Hostas have become and have been for some time eminently fashionable plants. Unfortunately, hand in hand with the improvement in and proliferation of hosta hybrids, there has arisen a perceived lowering of their value. Erstwhile enthusiasts murmur about there being too many new hostas, arbiters of taste hint at exaggeration of leaf size, and those imbued with a European idea of the appropriate find some of the new cultivar names almost impossible to take. This has not yet led to a general falling out of favour, but is almost certain to. Meanwhile, the suspense of perception that so often sustains fashions continues to operate.

The pursuit of fashion is inseparable from human nature. Although fashion is by no means always synonymous with beauty, so deeply ingrained is its importance that people have always been capable of suspending their mental censor in its cause. Built-up shoes like surgical footwear, collars starched like steel,

Hosta 'Blue Angel'.
Photo John Kelly.

Above far left: **Three seemingly identical hostas that have been given cultivar names. Top centre; 'George Smith', bottom left; 'Color Glory', and bottom right; 'Borwick Beauty'.**

Above left: **Hosta sieboldiana var elegans.**

Below, far left: **Hosta 'Snowden'.**

Below left: **Hosta montana 'Praeflorens'.**

Photos John Kelly.

augmented busts, busts bound flat, wigs, corsets, macassar and waspies, all have involved the sacrifice of comfort and natural appearance on the altar of fashion.

Horticulture is far from immune to the vagaries of fashion. Whole genera can enjoy periods of almost universal acclaim, only to pass away beneath the frowns of the trend-setters. Ferns were immensely popular once upon a time, show auriculas were *le dernier cri* at one level, while it was double primroses at another; and social distinctions restrict the appeal of dahlias, chrysanthemums and brightly coloured annuals.

It would be a shame if hostas were ultimately faced with ostracism. They are among the most superb of our garden plants, yet have within their ranks all the flaws and vulnerabilities that must inexorably lead to a fall from their present status as fashionable plants. For instance, the fact that they are easily bred has inevitably led

to there being a great many cultivars, by no means all of which deserve distinction. Hostas are essentially somewhat flamboyant, while at the same time having a propensity for modesty – and it is their flamboyance that is taken up by the fashionable. A great many of the most successful new hybrids come from America – so they are immediately easy targets of prejudice. And worst of all, some have been given unquestionably vulgar names – which means that no matter how beautiful they are they will be swiftly cast out by fashion's arbiters. Hostas are balanced on the twin knife-edges of appearance and language – the Scylla and Charybdis of fashion.

Perhaps for some of the modern cultivars it may be no bad thing, but the danger lies in throwing out the baby with the bath water. It will be hard to blame anyone for dissociating themselves from plants with egregious names like 'Yellow Splash Rim', 'High Fat Cream',

'Green Piecrust' and 'Chartreuse Wiggles'. It will certainly be necessary to do something about a situation in which three differently named cultivars are, as far as the eye can tell, identical. Unfortunately, fashion being what it is, eminently respectable, distinctive hostas with socially unexceptionable names are all too likely to receive the cold shoulder as well. This must not be allowed to happen.

The National Collection of hostas is in half-a-dozen distinct hands. Among them, Ann and Roger Bowden have a specific responsibility for modern hybrids. They are down-to-earth people, neither given to pursuing trendiness nor to condemning plants for something that is not inherently a horticultural fault. They are people of judgement and sensibility, however, and it is not for nothing that they are one of the very few husband and wife teams to be Joint Registrars for Britain for a genus of plants.

There is very little chance of any hosta – species or hybrid – becoming endangered while they have anything to do with it, as long as it displays garden-worthiness and is not eventually shown to be identical to another already in existence. When the hosta penny drops, and the collective back is turned on these noble plants, time and the National Collection system will quietly care for a living archive from which they can emerge again when it all blows over.

This is a perfect illustration of the *raison d'être* of the National Collections. It is far too late to act once the nation's gardeners have taken their dismissive spades to suddenly un-fashionable plants. It must have happened over and over again in years gone by, although probably not nearly as quickly. Nowadays a sneer from an influential source, 'Not helle-bores, surely, darling!' runs like fire through

Hosta '**Green Fountain' in the foreground. Behind it is *H.* 'Halcyon'.**
Photo John Kelly.

Left: **Hosta 'Devon Blue'.**
Photo John Kelly.

Below: **Hosta 'Frosted Jade'.**
Photo John Kelly .

Hosta 'Halcyon'.
Photo John Kelly.

Hostas in a corner of the Bowdens' garden: centre, 'Gold Standard'; to its right in picture, 'Blue Moon'; bottom right, 'Happiness'.
Photo John Kelly.

gardening's communications network; in former days it no doubt took longer but was just as effective – the Ellen Willmotts of that world were by no means exclusively positive in their influence. Those who, like the Bowdens, care for the plants for their own sakes and not for their popularity, provide insurance against the day when the bath is emptied, whether the emptying is gradual or overnight.

It is quite surprising, as one travels about meeting people who run nurseries, how many of them had other occupations first. Britain and Ireland have always been the cradle of the amateur; now they seem adept at producing the neophyte professional – self-trained, dedicated, level-headed and extremely efficient. Again and again one meets National Collection holders who have succeeded or even excelled in other professions, only to abandon them for trading in plants. Sometimes, as with Peter and Susan Lewis, who look after campanulas near Cambridge, the collection came first and gave birth to the nursery; with others, such as the Bowdens, it was the other way round.

However, they were not nursery people at all at first, but ran a thriving transport business from their home in Devon, contracting, among other things, to haul timber for the Forestry Commission. Only since March 1992 have they devoted themselves full time to their business in hostas; it took 35 years for the plants finally to oust the heavy plant.

Now the Bowdens' hosta nursery is a model of horticultural excellence. Hostas are not easy to manage on a large scale; they take up a lot of room and some can be just a little fussy about soil and temperature. Most require shade unless they can have a constantly moist soil, and shading a very large number of plants efficiently is neither cheap nor simple.

Although they have this requirement for shade, too much of it will draw the plants up out of character and lead toward their becoming more vulnerable to pests. It is quite easy to manage part shade for the few that most of us can accommodate, but takes considerable organisation on a nursery scale.

However, as Ann says, 'Sissinghurst has walls, Hidcote has hedges; we have roads and lanes'. Their property is made up of parcels here and there near their main garden, but even that is in two halves, one on either side of the road through the village. A couple of bends of a Devon lane, past the old carpenter's shop where Roger watched the work as a boy, and you find yourself in an entirely modern shade-yard, with hostas planted in neat blocks, green-leaved, grey, blue, variegated, gold, tiny and plantain-like, or enormous and wrinkled like the shoulders of an elephant. The Bowdens' series of comparatively small, sheltered sites is ideal for the production and growing-on of plants, as well as being reassuringly attractive.

There are plants to suit all tastes, with the actual leaf sizes varying from 2.4cm (1in) to 45cm (18in). The established clumps may be anything from 4.8cm (2in) high to 90cm (3ft). Really large hostas, such as 'Snowden' are entirely capable of being 2.4m (8ft) across and occasionally flowering stems will grow as tall as

The perfect setting in which to study hostas and the conditions they like best.
Photo John Kelly.

1.5m (5ft). Hostas are flowering plants, but until recently the flowers have been thought of almost as an embarrassment compared to the beauty of the leaves. That is changing, too, as American and Japanese hybrids are raised whose flowers are a match for many a lily, both in size and fragrance.

You should not think that hostas are difficult; they are not. They are good-tempered plants that merely demand a little extra care. Their Japanese homes vary greatly in their climates, and some hostas will do better in yours than others, but once they become established they are reliable fixtures. Many, but not all, will grow in full sun in moisture, but it is as well to be told that white variegation tends to burn, whereas yellow-patterned leaves are not nearly as susceptible to damage.

Arum lilies (*Zantedschia aethiopica*) with *Hosta sieboldiana* var *elegans*.
Photo John Kelly.

Ann's and Roger's business is made less seasonally hectic than many other nursery endeavours because hostas are so accommo-dating that they can be lifted and despatched by post at any time of year, even in the middle of summer. It is just as well, as the amount of plant material they send out in a year is very large and increasing all the time. Somehow they manage to fit in their responsibilities as genus registrars, and Roger, typical of those busy people whose time seems to have a flexibility denied to most of us, is Secretary of the Hosta and Hemerocallis Society.

Not bad for a couple who started with three plants grown for flower arrangement! A local general nurseryman who grew about twenty different hostas sadly died, and rather than see the stock dispersed, the Bowdens bought the lot. From that acorn a fine tree has grown, and this corner of Devon, where you will also find gentle humour and delicious chocolate cake, is a centre for horticultural excellence unencumbered by the whims and fancies of fashionable gardening.

A Note on Photographing Plants in National Collections

Some of the National Collections are photographed by professional photographers. Some of the professionals are expert plantsmen; some are not. The photographic archives of other collections rely on amateurs; some of them are expert photographers, others are not. Still other collections are barely photographed at all.

During the course of the research for this book, I have had the opportunity of looking at many National Collection archive photographs. In many cases the standard of photography has been very good, with sharp detail and informative content. In far too many others, however, badly blurred images, almost complete lack of depth of field, flowers isolated from any sense of scale, and poor colour rendition have rendered the pictures quite useless.

It is highly desirable that the collections should all be recorded by means of photographs if at all possible. However, 'recorded' is the operative word. Pictures of a flower head alone are insufficient if the subject is a member of a group of plants that vary in height, habit or foliage, and tell you nothing about the floriferousness – the sheer amount of flowers – that a plant bears. There should always be some sense of scale, although sometimes this is not possible. Flower stem pictures are much more effective if, as in Philip Vlasto's studies of salvias, an actual scale is included in the picture. Often the sense of scale is given by the very fact that the plants are familiar and everyone has an idea of their size, but that is not reliable of course.

Wherever it can be managed, plants should be photographed in context as well as portrayed as individuals. In photographing National Collections this might not be thought of as important, and an assumption is often made that, as the pictures are primarily for the use of people who already have some knowledge of the genus concerned, a series of plant portraits is all that is required. This is a mistake. Again to refer to *Salvia*, there would be no way of knowing, without a context picture and with only plant portraits, that *S. patens* is about 35cm (1ft 2in) high, while *S. concolor* (whose flowers are of a similar size and shade of blue) can attain heights of 2.4-2.5m (8-10ft) in the open in mild parts of Britain.

Scale and context are subtle matters. It only needs a plant or other relevant object whose parameters are universally familiar to appear in the picture for the scale to be established immediately. A clump of snowdrops, a crocus, a delphinium, or even the fallen leaf from an oak tree will allow the eye to interpret the scale without difficulty. There is no reason, when pictures are taken purely for the archive, why the labels – which provide scale as well as identity – should not be included. Publishers of books and magazines do not like them, however, and as collection holders may be asked (as some have been in the preparation of this book) to provide photographs for publication, it is better to remove the labels. However, the greatest care must then be taken to ensure that the subjects correspond to the pictures. This is a more difficult task than you might think; human memory is overestimated, particularly by the individual concerned, and the best way is to take notes, preferably with a view to matching the numbers in your notes (shot 5: *Geranium* 'Wargrave Pink') to the frame number that will appear at the side of the negative or transparency. It will mean mounting your own slides, but that is not a troublesome task.

Sharpness is vital in plant photography. The information given by a blurred photograph is minimal, to say the least, and fuzzy pictures are hard on the eyes. If you want to be able to determine the number of stamens (important in some rhododendrons, for example), you will be hard pressed to do so if the picture is less than pin sharp. Furthermore, as much of the picture as possible should be sharp, not just one sector of detail, and that means obtaining the maximum depth of focus (depth of field).

Where colour is important, as it usually is in collections of cultivars, and where colour variants of species are prized, the quality of incident light and the characteristics of the film should be taken into consideration, as either will cause an apparent colour shift under differing conditions.

Firstly, though, let us dismiss any lurking

suspicion that you need a 'posh' camera. It is best to use a single lens reflex (SLR) camera, rather than a fully automatic snapshot camera, as you will want to control certain functions in the interest of sharpness. However, entry-level SLR cameras are not expensive, and you do not need the array of lenses that might be presented to you as desirable. The standard 50mm lens will do just about all the jobs you want to do, but a 35-70mm zoom lens is especially suited to photographing in gardens, as you can frame your pictures properly without having to step on flower beds. This is highly important in other people's gardens.

I use two Canon SLRs in the EOS range, and am not one to decry autofocus, as most professionals do. The key to using autofocus is to use it intelligently, and it is a boon to people whose eyesight is not brilliant, which means most people over forty years of age. If the autofocus is being 'fooled' by what is in front of the lens (and it happens seldom), then there is usually a facility for switching to manual focus.

I also have a Bronica ETRS medium-format camera that takes 6 x 4.5cm transparencies. This is a comparatively large, heavy camera and rather expensive, and the reason I use it is to obtain for publication enlargements bigger than the 35mm format will allow even from the best quality slides. It has manual focus only. My wife does not share my feelings about autofocus (she is much

younger than I am), and her 35mm camera is a Nikon F3, a model much used by professional photographers in all fields.

What she and I agree on, however, is the absolute necessity for using a tripod for plant photography. The reason has everything to do with sharpness. Obviously, a firm tripod greatly diminishes camera shake. If you want to abolish it altogether, make sure you buy a camera that can be used with a cable release. Some men are loth to admit that they may cause camera shake, priding themselves in the steadiness of their hands and heartbeats. Machismo is a great deceiver, especially when combined with lack of objectivity in assessing one's own work.

However, there is more to lack of sharpness than camera movement. In order to obtain good depth of field, you need to use as small an aperture as possible, and this means employing a slower shutter speed than you might otherwise choose. The slower the shutter speed, the more any movement will blur the picture. Plants move quite a lot, sometimes in the lightest of airs, and any movement while the shutter is open will cause a badly blurred picture. Successful plant photography depends on your being patient. I once waited for forty minutes in Beth Chatto's garden for a plant of *Dierama pulcherrimum* to come to rest. It never did, and I gave up on the shot rather than speed up the exposure in order

A sturdy tripod and cable shutter release allowed this picture of *Passiflora vitifolia* to be taken in a greenhouse at dusk without colour distortion and without the use of flash. Canon EOS 620, eight seconds at f11, Fujichrome RDP 100.

Photo John Kelly at Reads Nursery.

to 'freeze' the movement. The result would have been a shallow, meaningless picture in which only one or two of the several 'fairy fishing rods' would have been in sharp focus, and the *Rosa glauca* behind them, whose foliage echoed the flower colour of the *Dierama* – the whole point of the picture – would not have been seen at all.

I almost always set the aperture at f16 for plant and garden photography. In very bright light I close it right down to f22, and it is only ocasionally, when light levels are really low, that I revert to f11. If f8 or wider is called for, I don't take the picture. If these standards mean shutter speeds of a quarter of a second, so be it.

Depth of field is one of the things that distinguishes good pictures from bad ones. Try if you can always to focus one third of the way into your subject, unless you are in close up, in which case it should be half. In practice, and especially with the Bronica, I often work away with the focus ring until I can see that the greater part of the picture as a whole is in focus, and then rely on depth of field to do the rest.

It is tempting, too, to use a fast film. Try to overcome the temptation, as the faster the film is, the grainier the picture and the less the detail will be resolved. I use ISO 100, and some professionals think that is too fast.

Different makes of film have different colour biases. This is because film can never be absolutely accurate, so each firm makes a judgement as towards which colour they will adjust their product. Some firms use stronger dyes than others, so the actual saturation of colour varies as well. Fujichrome is excellent for garden and plant photography, as it is faithful to greens, does not distort reds, and has good colour saturation. Kodak is a good compromise; Agfa tends to impose a pinkish aura, and one or two others give the effect of a blue or green wash.

You can get colour distortion in pictures taken in dark conditions, especially with exposures of more than a quarter of a second. When light is poor, you will have to sacrifice depth and open the aperture, otherwise the shutter speed will be so slow that there will be reciprocity failure. This shows itself in a colour shift due to the reciprocal ratio of shutter speed to aperture breaking down at slow speeds; the three emulsion layers, each of which is sensitive to a different colour, react differently to it. Nevertheless, if you have only one chance at a picture of a rarity, take it and see what happens – you never know how lucky you may be. For example, the picture of a scarlet passion flower on the page opposite was taken at dusk in a greenhouse at Reads Nursery (see page 120) with the aperture set at f11 and an exposure of eight seconds.

Incident light makes a big difference to colours. The light at midday appears to bleach out colours, while that of late afternoon or early morning enriches them. If the sun is behind or to one side of the camera, the colours will appear warm; if it is in front, they will be colder and altogether whiter, sometimes losing their colour entirely. Spring light is softer and more orange than summer light, which tends towards white and yellow; winter light has a blue cast. Colour trueness is more important in photographing National Collection material, especially cultivars, than in practically any other field of plant photography.

You can go to all the trouble in the world to get the colours right, only to have them ruined in the processing. Large establishments – more factories than laboratories – that churn out snaps of the Costa del Sol, Orlando and Skegness by the binful each summer are not the best places to entrust with your archive plant pictures. Tired chemicals and poorly adjusted conditions are not conducive to accurate colour rendition. It is far better to take them to a laboratory locally. If you happen to know someone who works on the local paper, ask them where the professional photographers take their work to be processed, and take or send yours there. You will find that a large number of keen amateurs do the same, and a member of your local amateur photographic society will also be a good person to recommend a laboratory.

Composition is a matter of aesthetics and is largely an individual matter. I am not an artist and therefore will confine myself to pointing out that plant photography for archive purposes should give as much information about the plants as possible. A picture of the flowers alone is often not enough unless you also have one of the entire plant, with its foliage, stems and flowers in focus and in proper proportion – that is to say not in a distorted perspective. A view from directly overhead is the least value of all, unless backed up by shots from other angles.

Photographing plants in the National Collections involves defining cultivars. It is usually the result of much study and knowledge and is therefore of the utmost value to those who follow. You cannot describe a cultivar adequately in words, but a photograph that shows every detail sharply, is true to colour, and shows all the characteristics of the whole plant, is a contribution to horticultural science.

Part 3

The National Collections' Gazetteer

The National Collections Scheme is not static. Collections change hands, fall temporarily into abeyance – as when a collection may have to be deemed to be not up to standard – or are accepted and added to the scheme. The information that follows was correct at the time of writing, but by and large there should not be too many radical changes in the years to come.

Unless an establishment is open to the public on a regular basis, precise addresses are not given. Should you wish to contact a particular collection holder, please apply to the NCCPG, The Pines, Wisley Garden, Woking, Surrey GU23 6QB (0483 211465), for a copy of their National Plant Collections Directory, which is revised annually. In the Directory, the number of species and cultivars is given for most genera. I have only given them if they are unexpectedly large or small.

Where the collection holder operates a commercial sales outlet, the entry below is marked with an asterisk (*). Mail order outlets are marked with two (**).

Here, as elsewhere in the book, 'variety' is used to denote cultivars as well as naturally occurring varieties, although the latter are occasionally written with the abbreviation var. and the varietal name in italics. The international definition of a cultivar is suspect and rightly the subject of controversy. Gardeners should take cultivars to be garden varieties propagated by means other than seed. This does not strictly accord with the international definition but is infinitely less confusing and much more applicable to gardening realities. Cultivar names are written in Roman lettering, with capital initial letters and single inverted commas, e.g. *Phlox* 'Kelly's Eye'.

ABELIA
Semi-evergreen or deciduous shrubs, hardy in the south and west. Bushy, with tubular funnel-shaped flowers.
Arts and Recreation Department, The Rotunda, Paignton, Devon.

ABIES
Conifers; the silver firs. They vary from tall, noble trees to very small, globular bushes suitable for the rock garden. Hardy, but they may be caught by late frosts.
Cairndow, Argyllshire, Scotland.

ABUTILON
The abutilons in cultivation are small trees and evergreen shrubs. The flowers of the latter are brightly coloured bells; in the former they are saucer-shaped. They are conservatory plants except in mild areas.
*Somerset College of Agriculture & Horticulture, Cannington, nr Bridgwater, Somerset. *
Bell-flowered: Goring-by-Sea, West Sussex.

ACACIA
The true acacias are very fast-growing trees from Australia with yellow pompoms in clusters. One species is the 'mimosa' of florists. All are tender;-outdoor cultivation is only possible in the mildest areas.
*Tresco Abbey Gardens, Isles of Scilly. *

ACANTHUS
Hardy herbaceous plants with conspicuously attractive leaves, more or less spiny. Spikes of flowers within spiny, hooded bracts.
Woolley Green, nr Bradford-on-Avon, Wiltshire.

ACER
The maple genus is a large one and is split between different holders. The National Collections, of which there are four, cover various sections of the genus. At Westonbirt Arboretum, near Tetbury, Gloucestershire, the collection consists of the Japanese cultivars. In north Lancashire it is restricted to cvs of *A. palmatum*, including many but not all Japanese maples. At Seaton Burn, near Newcastle upon Tyne, these are excluded, and at Hergest Croft Gardens, Kington, Hereford & Worcester, cultivars of *A. japonicum*, as well as *A. palmatum* play no part in the collection.

ACHILLEA
Hardy herbaceous perennials related to the native Yarrow. They have flat heads of tiny flowers in white, yellow and shades of pink and light red.
*Capel Manor Horticultural and Environmental Centre, Bullsmoor Lane, Enfield, Middlesex. ***

ACTINIDIA
Hardy, deciduous climbers, grown for their foliage, which is velvety in *A. chinensis* (the Chinese gooseberry or Kiwi fruit) and beautifully variegated in *A. kolomikta.* 6 species, 8cvs.
Bristol Zoological Gardens, Clifton, Bristol.

ADENOPHORA
Hardy herbaceous perennials that are not often grown due to being overshadowed by their close relatives, the campanulas. The flowers are mostly blue and open-bell shaped.
Padlock Croft, West Wratting, Cambridgeshire. *(See page 42). ***

AECHMEA
A genus of bromeliads, some of which are easy greenhouse or house plants. Some aechmeas are epiphytic, while others grow in soil. The collection, at 31 species and 12 cultivars is large, as only half a dozen aechmeas are general cultivation all told.
Liverpool City Council, Calderstones Park, Liverpool.

AESCULUS
There are 13 species of horse chestnuts in nature and, remarkably, the National Collection consists of nine of them plus 2 cultivars.
The Edward James Foundation, West Dean Estate, Chichester, Sussex.

AGAPANTHUS
Hardy and half-hardy perennials from South Africa in the lily family. The roots are fleshy and the plants are clump forming. The flower heads are large and the colour is generally in the blue range of the spectrum. The collection is notable for the large number of species and cultivars – 65.
Bicton College of Agriculture, East Budleigh, East Devon.

ALCHEMILLA
Hardy herbaceous perennials with beautiful foliage. Hairs on the leaves trap droplets of water and a jewel-like effect is created in

sunlight. Much used by flower arrangers.
Botanic Garden, University of Cambridge, Bateman Street, Cambridge.

Allium **'Purple Sensation'.**
Photo John Kelly.

ALLIUM
The ornamental onions are becoming recognised as including some of the best summer border plants, as well as alpines of distinction and, sometimes, elegance.
Caversham, nr Reading, Berkshire.

ALNUS
The collection is in the hands of two holders. There is considerable duplication but it is no bad thing where one has 25 species and 3 cultivars and the other has 33 species and 19 cvs; the point being that there are only 35 species world-wide.
St Brelade, Jersey.
Seaton Burn, nr Newcastle upon Tyne.

ALSTROEMERIA
Herbaceous perennials from South America. There have been great advances in breeding alstroemerias in recent years. Most are florists' flowers, but there are hardy plants, notably the Ligtu hybrids. 25 species, 56 cultivars.
*Spalding, Lincs. ***

AMELANCHIER
A genus of quite small trees, of which the most well known is *A. lamarckii,* the Snowy Mespilus. The collection of 8 species and cultivars is almost comprehensive in cultivation terms.
Durham, County Durham.

AMPELOPSIS AND PARTHENOCISSUS

The differences between the 'true' and 'false' Virginia Creepers are not often appreciated, and these genera warrant study side by side. Perhaps it is a little far for many people to go, but students should make the trip if possible.
Arduaine Gardens, Arduaine, Argyllshire.

ANEMONE

The anemone collection is divided into the Japanese anemones (*A.* x *hybrida*) and cultivars of *A. nemorosa*, the wood anemone. The Japanese anemones are in three separate hands. For one garden to have all of them would be to unbalance it, as these anemones are tall and flower in autumn.
Japanese anemones: Southampton; Hadlow College of Ag and Hort, nr Tonbridge, Kent; Danbury, nr Chelmsford, Essex.
Anemone nemorosa: The National Trust, Cliveden, Berks.

AQUILEGIA

A large genus of border and alpine 'Granny's Bonnets'. They hybridise with ease and it is a major undertaking to keep the 65 species and 55 cultivars of the collection true. Some of the alpines have suffered badly from impostors.
Fen Ditton, Cambridgeshire.

ARABIS

There are over 120 species of arabis world wide, consisting of hardy annuals and evergreen, usually low perennials. Only a minority are of garden merit.
Stockwood Country Park, nr Luton, Bedfordshire.

ARACEAE

This is the Latin name for the arum family. The collection includes the hardy members, with the exception of *Arisaema* and *Zantedeschia*. Hardy genera in this family include *Acorus*, *Arisarum* and *Arum* . 74 species, 7cvs.
nr Taunton, Somerset.

ARBUTUS

There are two collection holders, one of which specialises in *Arbutus unedo* only, while the other covers the genus as a whole. These are the strawberry trees.
Marden, nr Tonbridge, Kent (Arbutus unedo) *(See page 74)*
The National Trust, Dunster Castle, Somerset.

ARGYRANTHEMUM

A genus of plants closely related to *Chrysanthemum*. Until recently it was in part included in the latter. It includes well known garden plants such as *A. foeniculaceum* (ex-*Chrysanthemum*) and 'Jamaica Primrose'.
Somerset College of Ag and Hort, Cannington, nr Bridgewater, Somerset.*
Also a private collection in Porlock Weir, Somerset.

ARTEMISIA

Artemisias are hardy or half-hardy herbaceous perennials and shrubs or sub-shrubs that are usually semi-evergreen. 'Hardy' is a relative term. They are grown for their foliage, which ranges from silver-grey to white. 70+ species, 20+ cultivars.
Elsworth, nr Cambridge.

ASTER

The aster collections are concerned with species and cultivars that comprise the Michaelmas daisies.
The Picton Garden, Malvern, Hereford & Worcs. (See page 115). 260 species and cvs. **
The National Trust, Upton House, Banbury, Oxon. 104 species and cvs.
Also collections near Bristol (300) and Leeds (141) Novi-belgii asters only.

ASTILBE

Hardy herbaceous perennials with plumes of tiny but vivid flowers in late summer. A large number of cvs have been raised in Germany. The foliage is attractive all season.
The Lakeland Horticultural Society's Garden, Ullswater Road, Windermere, Cumbria. 14 spp, 135 cvs.
Marwood Hill Gardens, Barnstaple, Devon. *

Astilbes.
Photo John Kelly.

AUBRIETA
Of the eighty aubrieta cultivars one National Collection has 36. It also has 7 species. The other has 72 and 3 species. In garden terms the species are of greatest importance as a gene pool.
Botanic Garden, University of Leicester, Oadby.
Stockwood Country Park, nr Luton, Bedfordshire.

AZARA
There are ten species of these evergreen shrubs from Chile and Argentina. The National Collection has nine of them plus three cultivars. They have richly fragrant, small, acacia-like, orange-yellow or yellow flowers.
University of Exeter, Main Estate, Exeter, Devon.

BAMBOO
The bamboos are undergoing almost constant revision, with species being allocated to different genera at such a rate that the whole group is as it were on shifting sands. For this reason it is excellent that one particular collection holder is able to look after bamboos as a whole. The genera are as follows:
ARUNDINARIA Drysdale Nursery, Fordingbridge, Hampshire. * *
CHUSQUEA Drysdale Nursery.
PHYLLOSTACHYS Drysdale Nursery & a collection in West Sussex.
SASA Drysdale Nursery & David McClintock, Sevenoaks, Kent – an international authority on bamboos.
BAMBOOS excluding PHYLLOSTACHYS & SASA University of Oxford Arboretum, Nuneham Courtenay, Oxon.

BEGONIA
There are two National Collections of *Begonia*. The cultivars of *B. rex*, a rhizomatous species with patterned leaves, are held separately from the more general collection.
B.REX cvs. Held at Stapeley Water Gardens, Nantwich, Cheshire (See page 23). * *
BEGONIA (General) Glasgow Botanic Gardens, Glasgow.

BELLIS PERENNIS cultivars
There are two main groups of these colourful perennials (biennials); the large-flowered Monstrosa varieties and the double miniatures, such as 'Dresden China'. They are descended from the common lawn daisy.
Shrewley, nr Warwick.

BERBERIS
This very large genus of shrubs is represented by only one National Collection, containing 33 species and 18 cvs. There are almost 200 in cultivation.
East Stoke, nr Newark, Nottinghamshire.

BERGENIA
The hardy evergreen perennials known as 'Elephant's Ears', highly valued for their large foliage, winter tints, and bright flowers in spring. The three collections have different emphases.
University of Cambridge Botanic Garden, Bateman Street, Cambridge. (8 species, 9 primary hybrids and 20 cultivars).
Maylandsea, Essex (5 species, 67 cultivars).
Cherry Hinton Hall Park, Cambridge City Parks, Cambridge (60 cultivars).

BETULA
To house large genera of medium-sized to large trees is only possible on large properties, which means that most are in institutional hands or on large estates. The birches are no exception.
Royal Botanic Gardens, Kew.
Wakehurst Place, Ardingly, nr Haywards Heath, West Sussex. (70 species, 16cvs)
Hergest Croft Gardens, Kington, Hereford & Worcs. 59 spp & cvs. *

BORAGO
Borage, the garden herb, is *Borago officinalis*. It was a surprise to the author, who knew of only 3 species and no cultivars, to find that the National Collection consists of 30 spp and cvs.
Chelmsford, Essex.

BORZICACTINAE
The name for a group of cactus genera from South America, including BORZICACTUS, MATACUNA, SUBMATACUNA, OROYA, AREQUIPA and AKERSIA.
Whitestone Gardens Ltd, Sutton, Thirsk, N. Yorkshire. * *

BRACHYGLOTTIS
This genus of New Zealand shrubs now includes all the shrubby senecios, so that, for example, the well known *S. greyi* and *S. monroi* now become *Brachyglottis greyi* and *B. monroi*.
Inverewe Garden, Poolewe, Achnasheen, Ross-shire.

BUDDLEIA

The popular garden buddleias are cvs of *B. davidii*, but there are many more species, several of which are first-class, if sometimes slightly tender.

Paignton Zoological Gardens, Paignton, South Devon. This collection excludes B. davidii. *41 species & 5 cultivars!*

A collection in Exeter of 40 cvs of B. davidii.

BUXUS

The National Collection of box has recently been augmented by the addition of an important commercial collection that developed from an amateur's deep interest.

The National Trust, Ickworth Park, Bury St Edmunds, Suffolk (6 spp, 75cvs).

*Langley Boxwood Nursery, Rake, Liss, Hants. 13 spp, 6 cvs. * ***

Also a collection in Bristol. 30 species and cultivars.

CALAMINTHA

Herbs related to mint and similar to basil and thyme. *C. clinopodium* is the wild basil or basil thyme – its flavour and scent are thyme-like.

Mark Place, Brenchley, Kent.

CALATHEA

House plants, closely related to *Maranta* and often sold under that name. In general the prettily patterned leaves are larger than in *Maranta*.

Liverpool City Council, Calderstones Park, Liverpool.

Calluna vulgaris 'Fire King'.
Photo John Kelly.

CALCEOLARIA

With something like 10 species, some primary hybrids and another ten or so cultivars – and this excludes the half-hardy biennials – the National Collection of 3 species and 4 cultivars has scope for extension.

Stockwood Country Park, nr Luton, Bedfordshire.

CALLUNA

The many varieties of ling, or true heather, belong to one species, *Calluna vulgaris*. There are two National Collections, one much larger than the other.

Harlow Carr Botanical Gardens, Crag Lane, Harrogate, North Yorks. 199 cvs.

*Royal Horticultural Society, Wisley Garden, Woking, Surrey. 568 cvs. ***

CALTHA

Hardy herbaceous, water-loving perennials; the marsh marigolds. There are 20 species, of which 17 are in the collection, along with 7 cultivars – a remarkable gathering of the genus.

nr Bridgwater, Somerset.

CAMASSIA

A genus of bulbs, producing 60-90cm stems, bearing light blue to blue-purple flowers in spring. Known as quamash.

*Apple Court, Hordle, Lymington, Hants. * ***

CAMELLIA

To take on a National Collection of camellias, of which the cultivars are countless, is a monumental task, but Mount Edgcumbe is famous for its camellias. It is not generally known that there are about 40 camellia species.

Mount Edgcumbe House and Country Park, Torpoint, Cornwall. 20 species, 450 cultivars.

CAMPANULA

*Lingen Nursery, Lingen, Bucknell, Shropshire. ***

*Padlock Croft, West Wratting, Cambridgeshire. (See page 42). 171 spp, 118cvs. * ***

CANNA

Tender herbaceous plants from Central and South America. Fiery colours in red, yellow and orange. Known as canna lilies or Indian shot.

The National Trust, Ascott, Wing, Leighton Buzzard, Beds.

CARPINUS

The collection is partly duplicated, with the larger one including hornbeam species as well

as cultivars; the smaller has cultivars (11) of the common hornbeam only.
The Sir Harold Hillier Gardens and Arboretum, Ampfield, Hants. Retail outlet; Hilliers' Nurseries, Romsey, Hants. **
Also a collection near Barnet, Hertfordshire.

CARYOPTERIS

Small, grey-leafed, blue-flowered, late flowering shrubs with aromatic foliage. They are not entirely hardy in cold areas.
Bristol Zoological Gardens, Clifton, Bristol.

CASSIOPE

Dwarf, evergreen shrubs related to heathers and requiring peaty, acid conditions and ample moisture. They are not very easy to grow.
The National Trust for Scotland, Branklyn Gardens, Perth.

CASTANEA

The genus includes 12 species of hardy deciduous trees and shrubs. *C. sativa* is the sweet chestnut and has a few cultivars, of which the best for fruit is 'Marron de Lyon'.
Kirkwhelpington, Northumberland.

CATALPA

Hardy deciduous trees with broad foliage and flowers like foxgloves, followed by long seed pods. *C. bignonioides* is the Indian bean tree from North America.
The National Trust, Cliveden, Berkshire.

CAUTLEYA

A small genus of perennials in the ginger family, flowering in late summer. Not entirely hardy.
nr Truro, Cornwall.

CEANOTHUS

A genus of shrubs, mostly from California but surprisingly hardy. There are evergreen and deciduous species and many cultivars. The flowers are usually blue but pink and white also occur.
South Devon Health Care, Torquay. 40 spp, 60 cvs.
Somerset College of Ag and Hort, Cannington, nr Bridgwater, Somerset. *
London SW1, 59 spp & cvs.
Dudley Metropolitan Borough Council, Stevens Park, Stourbridge, West Midlands.

CERATOSTIGMA

The hardy plumbagos are low growing shrubs or herbaceous perennials. The flowers are rich

blue and similar in shape to those of the true plumbago. They are hardier than generally supposed.
Wolfson College, Linton Road, Oxford.

CERCIDIPHYLLUM

One of the smallest National Collections, consisting of the only two species, one of which is regarded by some authorities as a botanical variety of *C. japonicum*, the Katsura tree. There are 3 cultivars of this species, only one of which, apparently, is in the collection. The genus is of interest as its botanical standing is highly tenuous.
nr Wimborne Minster, Dorset.

CHANAECYPARIS LAWSONIANA

This is just one of the species of false cypress. It has given rise to a very long list of cultivars, both tree-size and dwarf.
Botanic Garden, University of Leicester, Oadby.
Bedgebury National Pinetum, Bedgebury, Kent.
143 cultivars.

CHIONODOXA

A truly remarkable collection of this genus of small, hardy bulbs with star-shaped, six-petalled flowers, flowering early in the year. The 9 species are to be expected but the 110+ cultivars compare curiously with the half dozen or so in general cultivation.
Lasswade, Midlothian.

CIMICIFUGA

Medium or tall herbaceous perennials with attractive, divided foliage and bottle-brushes of flowers, usually white, in late summer and autumn.

Just one of the 450 camellia cultivars in the National Collection. Photo John Kelly.

Clematis montana* and *Acer palmatum atropurpureum.
Photo John Kelly.

A comprehensive collection of all the available species and cultivars, many of which are barely in cultivation.
Bridgmere Nurseries, Nantwich, Cheshire. *

CISTUS
Mediterranean shrubs of great beauty, having aromatic foliage, often grey, and flat flowers in red, pink and white. There are small and medium shrubs; the latter have very large, papery flowers. Hardy in mild areas.
Chelsea Physic Garden, Royal Hospital Road, London.
Also a collection in Leeds.

Colchicums.
Photo John Kelly.

CITRUS
Reads Nursery, Lodden, Norfolk. (See page 120).

CLEMATIS
Treasures of Tenbury Ltd, Tenbury Wells, Hereford & Worcs. Over 200 species and cultivars. * *
The Guernsey Clematis Nursery Ltd, St Sampson, Guernsey.

CODIAEUM
Codiaeums are the house plants known generally as crotons. They are grown for their brightly patterned leaves and are not always easy to please.
Liverpool City Council, Calderstones Park, Liverpool.

COLCHICUM
The so-called autumn crocuses are not crocus and should not be confused with the plants that are and which belong in the genus *Crocus*. Many are easy to grow, but others are not, and could in the long term be lost to cultivation without proper care.
The Royal Horticultural Society, Wisley Garden, Woking, Surrey.
The National Trust, Felbrigg Hall, nr Norwich, Norfolk.

COLUTEA
A small genus of shrubs. *C. arborescens*, the bladder nut, is the only one at all widely grown. About six species are cultivated in Britain; three are in this collection.
London SW3.

CONIFERS (DWARF AND SLOW GROWING)
An extremely large collection of 314 species and 1892 cultivars, providing an unrivalled opportunity for study – essential for those who wish to know their ultimate dimensions.
Savill and Valley Gardens, Windsor Great Park, Berks. *

CONVALLARIA
There is one species of lily-of-the-valley and 9 cultivars. All are represented in the collection.
The National Trust, Cliveden, Berks.

COPROSMA
A genus of shrubs and small trees, mainly from New Zealand. Generally speaking, the coprosmas are of more botanical interest than horticultural.
Ventnor Botanic Garden, Ventnor, Isle of Wight (See page 48).

CORDYLINE

Tender, tree-like members of the agave family, related to *Dracaena*. The identity of specimens accredited to *C. australis* and *C. indivisa* is in doubt in some quarters. The 'Torbay Palms' belong to this genus.

*Somerset College of Ag and Hort, Cannington, nr Bridgwater, Somerset. ***

COREOPSIS

Hardy herbaceous perennials of the daisy family, with bright yellow flowers in summer.

Hardy Plant Society Botanic Garden, Nottingham.

CORNUS

The dogwoods belong in two main groups, the 'flowering' dogwoods from America, Japan and China, and those grown primarily for their brightly coloured winter stems and whose flowers are insignificant. *Cornus controversa* is a large, ornamental tree, whose variegated form is an outstanding small foliage tree.

The Sir Harold Hillier Gardens and Arboretum, Ampfield, Hants.
Newby Hall Gardens, Ripon, North Yorkshire.
RHS Garden, Rosemoor, Gt. Torrington, Devon.
CORNUS FLORIDA cvs. *Ashridge Management College, Berkhamsted, Herts.*
*Secretts Garden Centre, Godalming, Surrey. ***

CORTADERIA

Pampas grasses.

Stockwood Country Park, nr Luton, Bedfordshire.

CORYLOPSIS

Early flowering shrubs, with 'catkins' of yellow flowers on naked branches early in the year.

Bromsgrove, West Midlands.

CORYLUS

The species hazels are grown for their foliage and their catkins, which appear early in the year. There are many cultivars grown for their nuts. Broadly speaking they are cobnuts (*C. avellana*) and filberts (*C. maxima*).

The Sir Harold Hillier Gardens and Arboretum, Ampfield, Hants.
The Brogdale Horticultural Trust, Faversham, Kent.

COTINUS

There are three species of smoke bush and a handful of cultivars with names referring either to the colour of the smoky inflorescence or the foliage.

Exeter.

COTONEASTER

This large genus, so well known for berrying shrubs, is in the hands of four collection holders.

The Sir Harold Hillier Garden and Arboretum, Ampfield, Hants.
Calderdale Metropolitan Borough, Wellesley Park, Halifax, N Yorks.
Merrist Wood Agricultural College, Guildford, Surrey.
A private collection near Petersfield in Hampshire, with 293 species and 30 cultivars, is the largest by a considerable margin.

CROCOSMIA

Brightly coloured, late summer herbaceous perennials. They used to be called montbretias. Newport, Isle of Wight.

The National Trust, Lanhydrock Gardens, nr Bodmin, Cornwall.

Top: **Cornus alternifolia 'Argentea'.**
Photo John Kelly.

Above: **Cortaderia 'Sunningdale Silver'.**
Photo John Kelly.

Crocosmia
'Lucifer'.
Photo John Kelly.

Cyclamen
repandum.
Photo John Kelly.

CROCUS

Those who imagine that crocus are limited to the usual ones seen in spring may be surprised at the size of the National Collection.

The Royal Horticultural Society, Wisley, Woking, Surrey.

A private collection in Nottingham (C. chrysanthus cvs only).

Ray Cobb, Nottingham has the largest collection, with 124 species and 28 cvs, excluding C. vernus and C. chrysanthus (See page 37). Botanists recognise anything from 90 of the species.

CYCLAMEN

The national cyclamen collection is dispersed among members of the Cyclamen Society, who between them hold 50 species and cultivars. Another collection, near Chichester in Sussex, concentrates on the forms of *C. coum*, a very hardy species flowering between December and March.

Also a collection in Nottingham.

CYTISUS

The brooms other than *Genista*.

Northern Ireland Horticultural and Plant Breeding Station, Armagh.

DABOECIA

Daboecias are numbered among the heaths and heathers and have comparatively large flowers. There are two species; one from the Azores, the other from the Iberian Peninsula and parts of western Ireland. There are numerous cultivars.

RHS Gardens, Wisley, Woking, Surrey. *

DAHLIA

Dahlias occur in cultivation in very great numbers and each year some cultivars are lost while others are introduced. Divided among three or four separate collections, the National Collection is protected from untoward events *(See page 110).*

Dyffryn Gardens, Cardiff.
Capel Manor, Enfield, Middlesex.
Roundhay Park, Leeds.
Bodelwyddan Castle, St Asaph, Clwyd.

DAPHNE

Small shrubs, evergreen or deciduous, with deliciously scented flowers. Species bloom in succession from early spring to high summer and beyond.

*RHS Garden, Wisley, Woking, Surrey.**
Arlesford, Hampshire.
Northwick, Cheshire.

DELPHINIUM

It is most important that delphinium cultivars be kept going at a time when few are grown. Most garden delphiniums are from seed strains.

Temple Newsam Estate, Leeds. 100 cvs.

DENDRANTHEMA

The genus *Chrysanthemum* has recently undergone a drastic revision which has left few species within *Chrysanthemum* and which has ordained new genera or expanded other established ones at its expense. What we generally

understand as garden chrysanthemums are now within the genus *Dendranthema.*
Home Meadows Nursery Ltd, Martlesham,
*Woodbridge, Suffolk (*Dendranthema *x koreana –*
Korean chrysanthemums).
*Cambridge NCCPG. (*Dendranthema zawadskii *i.e*
Chrysanthemum rubellum *cvs.)*

DENDROBIUM

A large genus of orchids, consisting of almost 1000 species in the wild. They are mostly epiphytic and are tropical.
Liverpool City Council, Calderstones Park, Liverpool.
Glasgow Botanic Gardens, Glasgow.

DEUTZIA

A genus of popular hardy, summer flowering shrubs, usually with small, white flowers.
Leeds.

DIANELLA

Australian and Tasmanian, grassy-leaved evergreen perennials with sprays of starry, blue or white flowers followed by blue berries. Uncommon. Five species are in general cultivation. 12 species, 13 cvs.
East Budleigh, Devon.

DIANTHUS

There are something like 1000 cultivars among the pinks and carnations, as well as several species. The cultivars consist of alpines, such as 'Little Jock' and 'Oakington', old-fashioned pinks, modern pinks, Malmaison dianthus (such as 'Tayside Red'; they are very uncommon), border carnations, annual carnations, and perpetual-flowering carnations.
Leighton Buzzard, Bedfordshire (alpine dianthus).
*Shaugh Prior, Devon, (*Dianthus alpinus, callizonus,
gratianopolitanus *and* pavonius*) 4 species; 20+ cvs.*
Tetbury, Gloucestershire. (Malmaison) 5 cvs.
The National Trust for Scotland, Crathes Castle,
Banchory, Kincardine (Malmaison) 6 cvs.
Richmond Green, Surrey (old-fashioned pinks) 103
cvs.
Ross-on-Wye, Hereford and Worcs. (old-fashioned
pinks) 140+ cvs.

DICENTRA

Hardy perennials with arching sprays of locket-shaped flowers. Sometimes called 'Bleeding Hearts'.
Hardy Plant Society, Southern Counties Group. Held
on their behalf in Crawley, Sussex.
Also a larger collection near York.

Dendranthema **x** *koreana* **(Korean chrysanthemum) 'White Gloss'.**
Photo John Kelly.

DICKSONIACEAE

The genus of 'hardy' tree ferns within this family is *Dicksonia.* Two species are grown out of doors in Cornwall, the west of Scotland and the Republic of Ireland. Other species and genera are grown under glass.
Glasgow Botanic Garden.

DIERVILLA

A small genus of shrubs, related to *Weigela.* Most have yellow flowers. *D. middendorffiana* is usually sold as a weigela.
City of Sheffield Botanic Garden.

DIGITALIS

Foxgloves.
*The Botanic Nursery, Atworth, Melksham, Wilts. * **
NCCPG Warwickshire Group, Rowington, Warwick.
Tile College of Further Education, Coventry.

DODECATHEON

Pliny's name for the primrose, but applied to an American genus of woodland perennials with cyclamen-like flowers.
Walton-in-Gordano, nr Cleveland, Avon.

DORONICUM

Leopard's Bane. Several species of daisy-flowered herbaceous perennials, valued for their early flowering.
Baldersby, nr Thirsk, North Yorkshire.

DRACAENA

Palm-like plants, but related to agaves. Draceaenas are closely related to cordylines (q.v.) but are tender and make good house plants. *D. draco* is the Dragon Tree of the

Echeveria 'Silver on Red'.
Photo John Kelly.

Canary Islands.
Liverpol City Council, Calderstones Park, Liverpool.

ECHEVERIA
Easily grown succulents, often included in cactus collections but not related to them. They are cultivated mainly for their beautifully coloured leaves.
*nr Redhill, Surrey. **
Bunny, Nottingham.

ECHINOCEREUS
Easily grown cacti, hardy if kept dry in winter.
Swansea City Council.

ENKIANTHUS
Medium-sized, deciduous shrubs related to heathers. Grown for clusters of urn-shaped flowers and brilliant autumn colour.
*Glendoick Gardens Ltd, Glencarse, Perth, Scotland. ***

EPIMEDIUM
Hardy perennials, evergreen or semi-evergreen. Good flowering ground cover plants for part shade.
*RHS Garden, Wisley, Woking, Surrey. **
Also Acton Pigot, Shropshire.

ERICA
An extremely large genus, containing the great majority of the heathers.
The United Distillers (Bell's) National Collection, at Cherrybank, Perth, Scotland, is rightly celebrated and consists of no fewer than 1,000 cultivars.

*There is also a large collection at the RHS Garden, Wisley. **

ERIGERON
Small, daisy-flowered perennials and alpines.
nr Wotton-under-Edge, Gloucestershire.

ERODIUM
The Storksbills, relatives of the true geraniums. They are mostly rock garden plants.
Dumfries.
*R V. Roger Ltd., The Nurseries, Pickering, N Yorks. * ***

ERYNGIUM
Herbaceous perennials, many of which are hardy and ideally suited to maritime gardens. Known as the Sea Hollies.
nr Preston, Lancashire.

ERYSIMUM
In effect, perennial wallflowers. They are suitable for rock garden cultivation.
Wood Enderby, nr Horncastle, Lincolnshire.

ERYTHRONIUM
Very beautiful hardy bulbs. The flowers are shaped like the roofs of pagodas and are borne in spring. These American and Far Eastern plants have always been scarce but are now far more easily obtainable; and those who have kept them going in the past are greatly to be thanked.
Porlock, Somerset. 20 species, 12 cultivars.
Driffield, East Yorkshire. 25 spp, 18 cvs.

ESCALLONIA
Evergreen and deciduous shrubs from South America. The flowers are small bells in shades of red and pink or white. They are hardy near westerly and southerly coasts but need a warm wall inland.
University of Plymouth, Alston, nr Yelverton, Devon.
Northern Ireland Horticultural and Plant Breeding Station, Armagh.

EUCALYPTUS
The gum trees can only be propagated from seed and there are no cultivars. Their importance is increasing as strains from hardy provenances are becoming more readily available, and it is these upon which the National Collection is no doubt concentrating, following assistance from the CSIRO in Canberra.
Gatehouse of Fleet, nr Castle Douglas, Dumfries and Galloway.

EUCRYPHIA

Large shrubs or trees from Australia, Tasmania and South America. They are extremely beautiful when bearing their white flowers in late summer and early autumn.

Seaforde Gardens, County Down, Northern Ireland.

*The National Trust, Bodnant Garden, Colwyn Bay, Clwyd. * **

EUONYMUS

A large genus of trees and shrubs, including deciduous and evergreen species. Many of the former are notable for autumn colour. They vary as to hardiness. Some of the low-growing evergreens with colourful foliage make fine ground cover.

*Broadleas Garden Charitable Trust Ltd., Devizes, Wilts. **

*Merrist Wood College, nr. Guildford, Surrey. **

EUPHORBIA.

Abbey Dore Court Garden, Abbey Dore, Hereford & Worcs. (See page 000) *

University of Oxford Botanic Garden, Rose Lane, Oxford.

FAGUS

There are ten species of beech and about 40 cultivars.

Northumberland County Council. 28 spp & cvs. HRH The Prince of Wales, c/o NCCPG Wisley Gardens, Woking, Surrey. 8 spp, 44cvs

FERNS

There are a large number of ferns in cultivation in the British Isles. In addition to the many species there is a wealth of cultivars. In general, both species and cultivars are only reliably to be identified by experts, and without the National Collections scheme it is probable that, in time, many would be lost. The genera are:-

ADIANTUM. Maidenhair ferns: *The National Trust, Tatton Park, Knutsford, Cheshire.*

ASPLENIUM SCOLOPENDRIUM. Hartstongue fern: *The National Trust, Sizergh Castle, Kendal, Cumbria.*

ATHYRIUM. Lady ferns: *The Savill Garden, Windsor Great Park, Berks.*

CYSTOPTERIS. Bladder ferns: *Ludlow, Shropshire.*

DICKSONIACEAE. Tree ferns: *Glasgow Botanic Gardens.*

DRYOPTERIS. Buckler and Male ferns. *The National Trust, Sizergh Castle, Cumbria.*

FILICALES. General collections of hardy ferns: *Ottery St Mary, Devon (See page 93) and The Savill Garden, Windsor Great Park.*

OSMUNDA. Royal ferns: *Canley, Coventry.*

POLYPODIUM. Polypodies: *Harlow Carr Botanic Gardens, Harrogate, N. Yorkshire. Also nr Ludlow, Shropshire.*

POLYSTICHUM. The Shield ferns: *The Lakeland Horticultural Society, Windermere, Cumbria.*

THELIPTERIDACEAE. A family of ferns, including THELIPTERIS and PHEGOPTERIS: *nr Ludlow, Shropshire.*

FICUS

The edible figs only.

Reads Nursery, Loddon , Norfolk. (See page 120)

FORSYTHIA

These well-known, spring-flowering shrubs run to 6 species and 43 cultivars in the collection.

Droitwich, Hereford & Worcs.

FRAGARIA X ANASSA

Strawberries.

Brogdale Horticultural Trust, Faversham, Kent.

FRAXINUS

Species of ash are found over much of the northern hemisphere. The native British ash is *Fraxinus excelsior.*

Thorpe Perrow Arboretum, Bedale, North Yorkshire. 14 species, 7 cultivars.

Thornton Hall, Glasgow, 17 cultivars of F. excelsior.

FRITILLARIA

The fritillary genus is a very large one world wide, consisting of bulbs from every habitat from

Fritillaria meleagris.
Photo John Kelly.

Above: **Fuchsia**
'Mme
Cornelissen'.
Photo John Kelly.

Above right:
Garrya elliptica.
Photo John Kelly.

alpine screes to marshes. The many middle-eastern and American species are not represented.

Cambridge Parks Department, Cambridge. (F. imperialis cvs).
University of Cambridge Botanic Garden, Cambridge. (European species).

FUCHSIA (hardy)

University of Leicester, University Road, Leicester.
Croxteth Country Park, Liverpool.
Hatsford Fuchsia Collection, Ledbury, Hereford & Worcs.

GALANTHUS

Snowdrops. For those who imagine one snowdrop to be much like another, a visit to one of the National Collections would be a salutary experience.

RHS, Wisley. 28 species, 77 cultivars.
Collections in Hampshire and Shropshire.

GARRYA

A small genus of trees that bear 'tassels' of greenish flowers in the depth of winter.
National Botanic Gardens, Glasnevin, Dublin.

GAULTHERIA

The gaultherias are small, berrying shrubs belonging to the heather family. Recently, *Pernettya* became part of *Gaultheria*.
Porlock, Somerset.

GENTIANA ASCLEPIADEA cultivars

There are four cultivars of the willow gentian; 'Knightshayes', 'Nymans', 'Phyllis' and 'Rosea'.
Tewkesbury, Gloucestershire.

GERANIUM

It is always, unfortunately, necessary to define one's terms. *Geranium* is the genus to which belong the cranesbills, which are generally hardy plants. The greenhouse plants loosely called 'geraniums' belong to *Pelargonium*.

East Lambrook Manor, South Petherton, Somerset. 133 species, 157 cultivars (!)*
Cambridge Parks Department, Cherry Hinton Hall Park, Cambridge.
University Botanic Garden, Cambridge. 102 species, 24 primary hybrids.
Catforth Gardens, Catforth, Preston. *
Also a collection nr Billingshurst in West Sussex.

GEUM

Hardy herbaceous perennials for the border or rock garden.
Tiverton, Devon.

GLADIOLUS

Dudley Metropolitan Borough Council, West Midlands.

GLADIOLUS TRISTIS (Barnard Hybrids)

A unique and important collection of species and primary hybrid gladioli, which was assembled from South Africa by the late Professor Barnard, exists at his erstwhile home but its owner has elected to remain outside the National Collections scheme. Meanwhile, within it, there is a collection of some 25 hybrids of *G. tristis*.
Plant World Nursery, Gillingham, Dorset. *

GREVILLEA

Tender plants from Australia, related to proteas.

Some may be grown outside in very mild areas.
St Austell, Cornwall.

HALIMIUM
The collection of these sun-loving, small shrubs includes their hybrids with *Cistus*, which are designated x *Halimiocistus*.
Rawdon, Leeds.

HAMAMELIS
The well known, winter-flowering Witch Hazels.
Albrighton, West Midlands. 8 species, 48 cultivars.

HEBE
At present the National Collection of this very large genus of New Zealand shrubs concerns itself only with the more dwarf ones.
Hedgerow Nursery, Keighley, W. Yorkshire. 70 spp. & cvs.

HEDERA
The number of ivies in cultivation is truly vast.
Northumberland College of Agriculture. 800 cultivars (!!).
Erddig Hall Garden, Wrexham, Clwyd. about 100 spp & cvs.

HEDYCHIUM
The Ginger Lilies are among the most exotic-looking plants it is possible to grow out of doors in Britain and are spectacular in the conservatory in colder areas.
Hinton St George, nr Crewkerne, Somerset.

HELENIUM
Late flowering, floriferous herbaceous perennials, members of the daisy family and mostly American.
Canley, nr Coventry.

HELIANTHEMUM NUMMULARIUM cvs
These are the familiar helianthemums so often seen on rock gardens and known as Rock Roses.
Hampshire College of Agriculture, Sparsholt, nr Winchester. 80 cvs (!).

HELIANTHUS
The Sunflower genus, in which there are excellent herbaceous perennials.
The Hardy Plant Society Garden, Wollaton Hall, Nottingham.

HELICHRYSUM (dwarf varieties)
Exmouth, Devon.

HELIOPSIS
One of three summer-flowering, largely yellow, daisy-like herbaceous genera with similar names. The others are *Helenium* and *Helianthus*.
Hardy Plant Society Garden, Wollaton Hall, Nottingham.

HELLEBORUS
nr Salisbury, Wilts. (See p 79)
Also Hadlow College of Ag and Hort, Tonbridge, Kent.

HEMEROCALLIS
Day Lilies. This is one of the largest garden genera in terms of cultivars and has undergone rapid expansion in recent years. Those grown in Europe are almost all herbaceous; in hotter climates there are many evergreen Day Lilies.
The National Trust, Antony House, Torpoint, Cornwall. 400 cvs (!!).
Leeds. 4 species, 197 cultivars.
nr Ventnor, Isle of Wight. 102 miniature cultivars.

HEPATICA
Hardy woodland alpine plants related to buttercups but with blue flowers. Occasional cultivars are red or pink.
Plymouth, Devon. 4 species, 40 cultivars (!!!).
nr Harrogate, N Yorkshire. 35 spp & cvs.

HESPERIS
Sweet Rocket. One of the smallest collections (3 cultivars) but remarkable for one white form which was thought extinct.
Leicester University Botanic Garden, Oadby.

HEUCHERA
Hardy herbaceous, low-growing perennials with beautiful foliage, sometimes copper-purple, and sprays of small flowers that are excellent for cutting.
Colyton, Devon.

HIBISCUS SYRIACUS
Late-flowering shrubs. They are hardy, deciduous, and dramatic for a short flowering period but difficult to place among other plants.
*Notcutts Nurseries Ltd, Woodbridge, Suffolk. **

HOSTA
One of the most rapidly expanding and popular genera of plants. Hardy herbaceous subjects, grown mainly for beautiful foliage, but increasingly appreciated for their flowers.

Top: **Hydrangea 'Mme F. Riverain.** Photo John Kelly.

Above: **Iris iberica,** an Oncocyclus iris from Iran and Turkey. This group of irises is not represented in the National Collection, but perhaps one day. Photo John Kelly.

RHS Garden, Wisley. 202 species and cultivars. * *Harewood House Gardens, Leeds.* *Apple Court, Hordle, Lymington, Hants (small-leafed).* ** *Sticklepath, Devon. 36 species, 284 cultivars (!!). (See page 132)* ** *Further collections in Leeds and Glasgow.*

HOYA

This quite incredible collection of tender, evergreen trailing plants contains 200 species and cultivars. The total number of hoyas available in the trade is 24. The total number of species in the wild is 200.
The Welsh Mountain Zoo, Colwyn Bay, Clwyd.

HYACINTHUS ORIENTALIS

The common hyacinth.
Ripley Castle, nr Harrogate, N Yorks.

HYDRANGEA

Within their major groups – lacecaps and especially mopheads – hydrangeas are only distinguishable by their colour shades, which intensify, fade, or transmute according to soil conditions. The maintenance of accurate National Collections is a considerable undertaking and responsibility.
Derby City Council, Friar Gate, Derby.
Lakeland Horticultural Society, Windermere, Cumbria. 6 species, 144 cvs (!).

HYPERICUM

The St John's Worts vary from tiny, creeping plants to shrubs that are quite large. They all have yellow flowers, each with a conspicuous 'brush' of stamens.
Harlow Carr Gardens, Harrogate, N Yorks. 61 species, 15 cvs.
Royal Botanic Gardens, Kew (certain sections only) Wakehurst Place, Ardingly, Haywards Heath, West Sussex. 56 species, 15 cultivars.

ILEX

There are a great many species and cultivars of hollies, and National Collections are only possible in large, institutional gardens, especially as a good deal of work is being done on their taxonomy.
The Savill and Valley Gardens, Windsor Great Park, Berks. 44 species, 266 cultivars.
RHS Garden, Rosemoor, Great Torrington, Devon.

INULA

Hardy herbaceous perennials with large, daisy-like flowers. There are border plants and some suitable for the rock garden.
Knutsford, Cheshire.

IRIS

This is a very large genus indeed, consisting of dwarf, winter-flowering bulbs, tall water irises, the almost countless bearded irises, and many other different kinds. This is reflected in there being eight separate National Collections.
Bearded cultivars (award winning): *Myddleton House Garden, Enfield, Middlesex.* *
Iris ensata: *Marwood Hill Gardens, Barnstaple, Devon.* **
Series **laevigata** *except* **I. ensata:** *Hoxne, nr Eye, Suffolk.*
Iris sibirica: *Lingen, nr Bucknell, Shropshire.*
Species iris. University of Reading, Whiteknights, Reading, Berks.
Iris unguicularis: *Buckinghamshire. 15 cvs.*
Iris unguicularis & I. lazica: *Nr. Birmingham.*
Series **spuriae:** *Belsay, Newcastle upon Tyne.*

JASMINUM
Jasmines.
Arts & Recreation Department, The Rotunda, Paignton, Devon.

JUGLANS
Walnuts.
Thorpe Perrow Arboretum, Bedale, N. Yorkshire.
Also a collection near Wimborne in Dorset.

JUNIPERUS
The junipers are conifers and range from tiny cultivars suitable for troughs to tall trees.
Bedgebury National Pinetum, Kent. 32 species, 103 cvs.
Also a collection of prostrate forms at the Isle of Grain Power Station, Rochester, Kent.

KALMIA
Kalmias are shrubs, varying from alpines to large size, which are related to heathers and rhododendrons. They are very beautiful when in flower and have blooms like squared-off, doll's-tea-set saucers.
*Glendoick Gardens Ltd, Glencarse, Perth, Tayside. ***
*Kalmia latifolia: 'Secretts' Garden Centre, nr Godalming, Surrey. ***

KNIPHOFIA
The well known hardy herbaceous perennials often called 'red hot pokers'.
*Bridgemere Nurseries Ltd., Nantwich, Cheshire. ***
Also a collection on the Isle of Wight.

LAMIUM (including *Galeobdolon*)
Joe Sharman, Monksilver Nursery, Cottenham, Cambridge. (See page 32).
Also a collection in Walsall.

LATHYRUS
The best known species in this genus is *L. odoratus*, the annual sweet pea. However, the National Collection concerns itself with the perennial species and cultivars.
West Wickham, Cambridgeshire. 50 species, 34 cultivars.

LAVANDULA
It is not generally realised what a wide range of lavenders is available to gardeners. All the following have 50 or more species and cultivars.
*Norfolk Lavender Ltd, Kings Lynn, Norfolk. ***
*Jersey Lavender Ltd, St Brelade, Jersey. ***
Also a collection near Nottingham.

LEPTOSPERMUM
Tender shrubs or small trees in the myrtle family, with massed flowers like tiny dog roses. Natives of New Zealand but barely hardy in the south and west.
Southampton, Hampshire.

LEUCANTHEMUM X SUPERBUM
The border plant that used to be classified as *Chrysanthemum maximum*.
nr Wells, Somerset.
Mauchline, Ayrshire.

LEUCOJUM
Bulbs; the snowflakes.
Bradenham, nr High Wycombe, Buckinghamshire.

LEWISIA
Lewisias are alpine plants from America. They have flattish rosettes of fleshy leaves and sprays of highly colourful flowers. They are best

*Top: **Kalmia latifolia.***
Photo John Kelly.

Above:
Leptospermum 'Red Damask'.
Photo John Kelly.

Magnolia stellata.
Photo John Kelly.

grown in the alpine house or on their sides in rock crevices.
The National Trust for Scotland, Branklyn Gardens, Perth.
Sawbridgeworth, Hertfordshire (herbaceous lewisias only).
Dronfield, nr Sheffield, 140 species and cultivars (!)
Ashwood Nurseries, Kingswinford, West Midlands.

LIBERTIA
Somewhat tender, evergreen perennials, with a long season of flowering. They have erect flowering stems with long spikes of blooms which are usually white.
East Budleigh, Devon.

LIGUSTRUM
The privets.
The Sir Harold Hillier Arboretum, Ampfield, Hampshire.

LINUM
The National Collection of this genus, which includes commercial flax, amounts to 21 species and cultivars. There are 230 species in nature, but only a few are good garden plants.
Burnham, Buckinghamshire.

LIRIODENDRON
The tulip trees. There are 2 species and about 4 cultivars in existence.
Chichester, West Sussex.

LIRIOPE
Hardy evergreen perennials, a little like elongated muscari but flowering late in the year.
East Budleigh, Devon.

LITHOCARPUS
A genus consisting of scrubby oaks but distinct from *Quercus* in many aspects of the flowers (for example, the flower spikes are upright in Lithocarpus, pendulous in *Quercus*).
The Sir Harold Hillier Arboretum, Ampfield, Hampshire.

LOBELIA CARDINALIS AND L.FULGENS
nr Dorchester, Dorset. (See page 103).

LONICERA
This large genus includes the climbing honeysuckles as well as many small to medium-sized shrubs, including the well-known hedging plant, *L. nitida.*
Climbing honeysuckles: *J. Bradshaw & Son, Busheyfields Nursery, Herne Bay, Kent. 63 spp & cvs. ***
Species and primary hybrids: *University Botanic Garden, Cambridge.*

LUPINUS
The Russell lupins.
Albrighton, West Midlands.

LYCASTE AND ANGULOA
Two genera of fragrant, South American orchids, sufficiently closely related to have given rise to bigeneric hybrids. They do not require high temperatures but are susceptible to draughts. Moisture management requires care.
Beckenham, Kent. 230 species and cultivars (!!).

LYCHNIS
A genus of campions and catchflys.
West Ewell, Surrey.

LYSIMACHIA
Easily grown herbaceous perennials, including Creeping Jenny. Many have a tendency to be invasive.
Wolfson College, Oxford.
Evesham, Hereford & Worcs.

MAGNOLIA
Three superb National Collections cover the magnolias, among which exciting new cultivars are proliferating rapidly.
*The National Trust, Bodnant Garden Colwyn Bay, Clwyd * 30 spp, 47 cvs.*
*The Savill and Valley Gardens, Windsor Great Park, Berks. * 34 spp, 242 cvs.*
Tilgates, Bletchingley, Surrey. 336 spp & cvs.

MAHONIA

Hardy and near-hardy shrubs with dramatic, evergreen foliage and yellow flowers, for the most part borne in winter.
*Savill & Valley Gardens, Windsor Great Park, Berks. **
Wimborne, Dorset.

MALUS

The genus includes apples, cider apples and crab apples.
Brogdale Horticultural Trust, Faversham, Kent. 2,400 cvs (!!).
(ornamental malus) University of Manchester, Oxford Road, Manchester.
(ornamental malus) Hyde Hall Garden Trust, Chelmsford, Essex.

MECONOPSIS

The blue poppies (not all are blue!)
Durham College of Agriculture and Horticulture, Durham. (See page 85).

MENTHA

The mints.
Caernarfon, Gwynedd.

MONARDA

Leeds Castle, nr Maidstone, Kent. (See page 70).

MUSCARI

The Grape Hyacinths.
Boxford, nr Colchester, Suffolk. 23 spp & 11 cvs.

NARCISSUS

The genus in the wild is very large. Given the enormous numbers of cultivars, it is hardly surprising that the collections are held by institutions with plenty of space.
*Country Gardens Garden Centre, London Road, Windlesham, Surrey. 100 species, 2402 cultivars.**
Guy Wilson Introductions: *University of Ulster at Coleraine, County Londonderry. 1000 spp & cvs.*
Brodie Cultivars: *National Trust for Scotland, Brodie Castle, Moray. 134 cvs.*
Alec Gray Hybrids: *Broadleigh Gardens, Bishops Hull, Taunton, Somerset. 63 cvs. ***

NEPETA

Leeds Castle, nr Maidstone, Kent. (See page 70)

NERINE

Beautiful South African bulbs, flowering late in the year and needing a warm, sheltered position.

The collection, held in Worcestershire, appears remarkably to consist of 50 species and 750 cultivars. Authorities generally admit about 30 species, and *The Plant Finder* lists only 18 nerines as being available to gardeners, but botanical classification is always a matter of opinion. Mr. C.A. Norris, the holder of the collection, maintains that, "It depends on whether you are a 'splitter' or a 'lumper'."
Upton-on-Severn, Hereford & Worcs.

NERIUM OLEANDER

The number of cultivars of the oleander is rapidly increasing. The collection is held by Cambridge NCCPG but at the time of writing is not permanently housed.

NOTHOFAGUS

The Southern Beeches are trees from the south of South America and are analogous to but not congeneric with the Northern Hemisphere beeches (*Fagus* spp).
Tavistock Woodland Estate, Gunnislake, Cornwall.
Royal Botanic Gardens, Kew, Wakehurst Place, Ardingly, Haywards Heath, West Sussex.
Crarae Garden Charitable Trust, Crarae Gardens, Inveraray, Argyll.

NYMPHAEA

Water Lilies.
*Stapeley Water Gardens Ltd, Stapeley, Cheshire. (See page 23). ***

OENOTHERA

Evening Primroses; herbaceous perennials and alpines.
Westbury, Wiltshire.

Mahonia x *media* **'Winter Sun'.**
Photo John Kelly.

OLEARIA
A genus of New Zealand shrubs with daisy-like flowers, usually white but sometimes purple, and attractive, evergreen foliage.
Dublin County Council, Dublin, Republic of Ireland.
*The National Trust for Scotland, Inverewe Garden, Poolewe, Achnasheen, Ross-shire. ***

OPHIOPOGON
A small genus of grassy perennials with strap-shaped leaves, small flowers, and blue or black berries. Most are Japanese.
East Budleigh, Devon.

ORIGANUM
Aromatic plants, including culinary herbs.
Staplehurst, Kent.
*Hexham Herbs, Chollerford, Hexham, Northumberland.***

OSMUNDA
The Royal Ferns, from which osmunda fibre is derived, much to their disadvantage.
National Trust Garden, Sizergh Castle, Kendal, Cumbria. 5 spp, 4 cvs.
Coventry. 3 spp, 20 cvs.

OSTEOSPERMUM
These beautiful but rather tender perennials, which have elegant daisy-type flowers in soft but rich colours, have increased greatly in popularity in recent years.
Somerset College of Agriculture and Horticulture, Cannington, Bridgwater, Somerset. 2 spp, 21 cvs.

Osteospermum **'Whirligig'.** Photo John Kelly.

OURISIA
Low-growing but showy, moisture-loving alpines from the Southern Hemisphere.
The National Trust for Scotland, Inverewe Gardens, Poolewe, Achnasheen, Ross-shire.

OXALIS
As well as some of the most pernicious weeds that beset gardeners, there are some extremely beautiful plants for the rock garden.
Leighton Buzzard, Bedfordshire.

PAEONIA
Peonies have an extremely long history as garden plants and one of the collections reflects this. Included in the National Collections are herbaceous species and cultivars and 'tree' peonies.
Lydney, Gloucestershire: (pre-1900 and early post-1900 peonies)
The National Trust, Hidcote Manor Garden, Chipping Campden, Gloucestershire.
Also a collection in Scotland

PAPAVER
The National Collections of poppies (as opposed to *Meconopsis*, the Himalayan Poppies), consist of annuals, held by a major seed company, and Oriental Poppies, held by a college in Scotland.
Annuals: *Thompson & Morgan Ltd., Poplar Lane, Ipswich.*
Papaver orientale: *The Scottish Agricultural College, Ayr.*

PAPHIOPEDILUM
A genus of tropical slipper orchids, related to *Cypripedium* and requiring heat, shade and high humidity.
Liverpool City Council, Calderstones Park, Liverpool.
*Ratcliffe Orchids Ltd., Owslebury, Winchester.***

PARAHEBE
Hardy rock garden plants from New Zealand, either perennials or low shrubs.
*County Park Nursery, Essex Gardens, Hornchurch, Essex. ***

PASSIFLORA
Passion Flowers: climbers for conservatory, greenhouse or occasionally a warm wall outside.
*Greenholm Nurseries Ltd, Clevedon, Avon. ***

PELARGONIUM
The plants we usually call "geraniums" – not to be confused with Geranium *(See page 154)* – are zonal pelargoniums. The genus also in-

cludes regal pelargoniums.
*Fibrex Nurseries, Pebworth, Stratford upon Avon, Warwickshire. * ***

PENSTEMON
Hardy and half-hardy perennials, sub-shrubs and alpine shrubs with lipped, tubular flowers in many colours.
Dorset College of Agriculture and Horticulture, Kingston Maurward, Dorchester, Dorset.
The National Trust, Rowallan Garden, Ballynahinch, County Down.
*The National Trust for Scotland, Threave Garden, Castle Douglas, Dumfries & Galloway. **

PERNETTYA
Small or dwarf, berrying shrubs related to heathers and rhododendrons. This genus is now included in Gaultheria (page 154)
*The Savill and Valley Gardens, Windsor Great Park, Berks. **

PHILADELPHUS
Well known, scented, summer-flowering shrubs.
The Hollies Park, Weetwood Lane, Leeds. 45 spp, 62 cvs.

PHLOMIS
There are more than 100 species in this genus, but only a few are in cultivation. Among them is the Jerusalem Sage.
Westbury-on-Severn, Gloucestershire. 45 species and cultivars.

PHLOX
A large American genus consisting of tiny, mat-forming alpines as well as tall herbaceous plants.
Phlox paniculata *(border phlox): Temple Newsam Estate, Leeds.*
***Phlox excluding the above:** Wickhambrook, nr Newmarket, Suffolk.*

PHORMIUM
The New Zealand 'flaxes' – evergreen perennials with tough, highly fibrous leaves, but not always hardy.
Somerset College of Agriculture and Horticulture, Cannington, nr Bridgwater, Somerset.

PHOTINIA
Evergreen and deciduous shrubs. The garden photinias are principally grown for their rhododendron-like foliage.
The Sir Harold Hillier Arboretum, Romsey, Hampshire.
Also a collection near Canterbury in Kent.

PHYLLODOCE
Dwarf shrubs, related to heathers and requiring peaty, moist conditions.
*Glendoick Gardens Ltd., Glencarse, Perth. * ***

PICEA
A genus of conifers; the spruces.
Argyllshire.

Above left:
Phormium tenax and bergenias.
Photo John Kelly.

Above: **Penstemon 'Garnet'.**
Photo John Kelly.

Above: **Pleione bulbocodioides.**
Photo John Kelly.

Above right: **Pieris 'Forest Flame'.**
Photo John Kelly.

PIERIS
Dramatically beautiful shrubs, related to heathers and rhododendrons. The swags of white or pink flowers often accompany startlingly red new foliage in spring.
Swansea City Council. 42 spp & cvs.
Savill & Valley Gardens, Windsor Great Park. 10 spp, 86 cvs (!!)

PINGUICULA
"Carnivorous" plants, a few of which are native to Britain and Ireland, where they grow in peat bogs and other wet mountain places.
Sherborne St John, Hampshire.

PINUS
The pine genus. The National Collection does not include dwarf cultivars.
The Hillier Arboretum, Romsey, Hampshire.

PITTOSPORUM
New Zealand shrubs, usually grown for their foliage, which is much used by flower arrangers.
Bicton College of Agriculture, East Budleigh, Devon.

PLATANUS
Plane trees.
The National Trust, Mottisfont Abbey, Romsey, Hampshire.

PLATYCODON
Herbaceous perennials, closely related to campanulas.
Tewkesbury, Gloucestershire.
*Padlock Croft, West Wratting, Cambridge * * (See page 42).*

PLEIONE
A genus of terrestrial orchids, many of which are hardy and can be grown in the alpine house or a frame.
*Butterfields Nursery, Bourne End, Buckinghamshire. **

POLYGONATUM
The genus that includes Solomon's Seal.
Kings Lynn, Norfolk.

POLYGONUM
A genus of dock-like plants, many of which are very fine for the garden. It has recently been split into *Polygonum, Fagopyrum, Fallopia* and *Persicaria*, the last of which has the best garden plants.
Brentnor, nr Tavistock, Devon.

POPULUS
The genus of poplars.
Lackham College of Agriculture, Lacock, Wiltshire.
Forestry Commission Research Division, Surrey. 45 species, 409 cultivars (!!)

POTENTILLA

Potentillas may be alpines, herbaceous perennials or shrubs (*P. fruticosa*).
Herbaceous: *Longfield Nursery, Cleobury Mortimer, Shropshire. ***
P. fruticosa: *Saundersfoot Bay Leisure Park, Dyfed. Webbs of Wychbold, Droitwich, Hereford & Worcs ** *Cawthorne, nr Barnsley, W. Yorkshire. The National Botanic Gardens, Glasnevin, Dublin.*

PRIMULA

There are no fewer than thirteen National Collections of the genus Primula. It is a very large genus, divided into sections consisting of groups of plants with similar characteristics. The sections differ widely in their cultural requirements, and this accounts to a large extent for the diversity of the collections.
European species: *Shrewton, Wiltshire.*
P. allionii *(an alpine-house species):* *Edinburgh.*
Alpine auriculas: *Leeds and W. Midlands*
Double auriculas: *Lincs.*
Green and grey show fancy auriculas: *nr Chatham, Kent.*
Border auriculas: *Haverfordwest, Pembrokeshire*
Sections Capitatae, Cortusoides, Farinosae: *Plant World, Newton Abbot, Devon.***

Primula marginata: *Summerbridge, nr Harrogate, W. Yorks.*
Section vernales *(includes the primroses):* *Ashby-de-la-Zouch, Leics.*
Asiatic primulas: *by Aberfeldy, Perthshire.*

PRUNUS

The plum and cherry family includes the fruit trees as well as ornamental cherries and other flowering trees.
District of The Wrekin Council.
Cherries and Plums: *Brogdale Horticultural Trust, Faversham, Kent.*
Prunus serrulata: *Kilbirnie, Ayrshire.*
P. subhirtella *(Spring Cherry)* and P. speciosa *(one of the ancestors of the Japanese cherries):* *Handcross, West Sussex. 60 species and cultivars.*

PSEUDOPANAX

Ventnor Botanic Garden, Ventnor, Isle of Wight (See page 48).

PULMONARIA

The lungworts; low-growing, mostly evergreen perennials with leaves often spotted and patterned with silver. The flowers are pink, white or blue, somewhat like forget-me-nots.
Shillingfleet, York, N Yorks.

Far left: **Primula pulverulenta.**
Photo John Kelly.

Left: **Primula bulleyana** and **P. helodoxa.**
Photo John Kelly.

Bottom, far left: **Primula florindae 'Copper'.**
Photo John Kelly.

Bottom left: **Primula japonica.**
Photo John Kelly.

Prunus subhirtella 'Pendula' at the RHS garden, Wisley.
Photo John Kelly.

PYRACANTHA
Brilliantly berried shrubs, usually grown on walls.
Chelmsford, Essex.

PYRUS
The pear genus.
European, Asian and perry pears: *The Brogdale Horticultural Trust, Faversham, Kent.*
Pyrus *species:* *Shrewton, Wiltshire.*

QUERCUS
The oak genus.
The Sir Harold Hillier Arboretum, Ampfield, Hampshire. 139 species, 70 cultivars.
Thorpe Perrow Arboretum, Bedale, North Yorks.
Chevithorne Barton, nr Tiverton, Devon. 131 species.

RANUNCULUS FICARIA
Surprisingly, there are 37 forms of the Lesser Celandine in this National Collection.
Bradenham, nr High Wycombe, Buckinghamshire.

RHEUM
There are spectacular ornamental rhubarbs as well as many culinary varieties such as 'Harbinger' and 'Timperley Early'.
Harlow Carr Gardens, Harrogate, N Yorks. 30 species, 115 cultivars.
Culinary rhubarb: RHS, Wisley. 2 spp, 64cvs.

RHODODENDRON
As with *Primula*, there are many sections in *Rhododendron*, but it needs a great deal more room because of the size of the plants, some of which are in fact trees. Accordingly, there are 14 separate collections, almost all of which are held by institutions.
Azaleodendron: *Burghclere, nr Newbury, Berkshire.*
***subsection* Barbata:** *The National Trust for Scotland, Inverewe Garden, Poolewe, Achnasheen, Ross-shire.*
***subsection* Falconera:** *Swansea City Council, West Glamorgan.*
***subsection* Falconera:** *Northern College, Wentworth Castle, Stainborough, S. Yorks.*
***subsection* Falconera:** *The National Trust for Scotland, Brodick Castle, Isle of Arran.*
R. forrestii: *The National Trust, Bodnant Garden, Colwyn Bay, Clwyd.*
Ghent azaleas: *The National Trust, Sheffield Park Garden, Uckfield, East Sussex.*
Glenn Dale Azaleas: *Savill & Valley Gardens, Windsor Great Park.*
***Subsection* Grandia:** *The National Trust for Scotland, Brodick Castle, Isle of Arran.*
Knaphill, Exbury and* Occidentale *azaleas: *Haywards Heath West Sussex.*
The Wilson 50 Kurume azaleas: *Department of National Heritage, Richmond and Bushy Parks, Richmond, Surrey.*

Subsection Maddenia: *The National Trust for Scotland, Brodick Castle, Isle of Arran.*
Species rhododendrons: *Savill and Valley Gardens, Windsor Great Park. 509 species.*
Subsection Triflora: *Swansea City Council.*

RHUS
Hardy deciduous shrubs and small trees with brilliant autumn colour.
Exeter, Devon.

RIBES
The genus that includes currants and gooseberries, as well as some ornamental shrubs.
Fruiting cultivars: *Brogdale Horticultural Trust, Faversham, Kent. 350 cvs.*
Species and primary hybrids: *University Botanic Garden, Cambridge.*
Gooseberries: *University of Manchester, Oxford Road, Manchester.*
Gooseberries: *Rougham Hall Nurseries, Rougham, Bury St Edmunds, Suffolk. **

RODGERSIA
Large-leaved, moisture loving perennials with long plumes of starry flowers.
Ilfracombe, Devon.
Castle Cary, Somerset.

ROHDEA JAPONICA
A perennial species, abstruse in the extreme, of which the collection holders are the sole source of supply. Of the twelve cultivars in the collection, none is available in the nursery trade or mentioned in the literature. A collection of marginal importance.
Apple Court Nursery, Hordle, nr Lymington, Hampshire. * *

ROSA
There are six National Collections of roses. For modern roses there is no better study centre than the Gardens of the Rose – the headquarters of the Royal National Rose Society at St Albans, Hertfordshire, although there is no National Collection as such.
19th century shrub roses: *The National Trust for Scotland, Malleny House Garden, Balerno, Midlothian.*
Rambling roses: *Woodmancote, nr Cirencester, Gloucester.*
The History of the European Rose: *University of Birmingham (See page 52).*
Pre-1900 shrub roses: *The National Trust, Mottisfont Abbey, nr Romsey, Hampshire (See page 62).*

Species roses: *Peter Beales Roses, Attleborough, Norfolk. * **
Rosa pimpinellifolia: *Lanarkshire.*

ROSCOEA
Hardy herbaceous plants with large, orchid-like flowers.
nr Truro, Cornwall.

ROSMARINUS
Rosemary – hardy and half-hardy evergreen shrubs.
Bridgwater, Somerset.

RUBUS
The genus to which brambles and raspberries belong.
Aberdeen College of Further Education, Aberdeen.

RUSCUS
Hardy evergreen sub-shrubs, including *R. aculeatus,* the Butcher's Broom. The National Collection consists interestingly enough of 9 species. Some authorities would limit the genus to 3, and others even to two by including *R. racemosa* in the genus *Danaë.*
University Botanic Garden, Cambridge.

SALIX
Willows.
Wolseley Garden Park, Stafford. 103 spp, 57 cvs.
Forestry Commission, Westonbirt Arboretum, nr Tetbury, Gloucestershire. 206 spp & cvs.
Dwarf species: *Northumberland County Council, Newcastle upon Tyne.*

SALVIA
Dorset College of Ag & Hort, Kingston Maurward, Dorset. (See page 107).

SAMBUCUS
Elders, many of which are first-class garden shrubs, notably when in flower and berry, although several are grown for their beautiful foliage.
The National Trust, Wallington Garden, Morpeth, Northumberland.
Also a collection in Strathclyde. 7spp, 25 cvs.

SANTOLINA
Hardy, evergreen, dwarf shrubs with aromatic, finely divided foliage and button-like, yellow flowers.
Herb and Heather Garden Centre, Selby, N. Yorks.
Tonbridge, Kent.

SARCOCOCCA
Evergreen, hardy shrubs with intensely scented, winter flowers.
Capel Manor Horticultural and Environmental Centre, Enfield, Middlesex.

SARRACENIA
Pitcher-shaped 'carnivorous' plants, relatively easily grown.
Bridgwater, Somerset.
Preston, Lancs.

SAXIFRAGA
A very large genus, but as they are nearly all small alpines a great many can be grown in a relatively small space.
European species: *University Botanic Gardens, Cambridge.*
Porophyllum section: *Waterperry Gardens Ltd, Wheatley, Oxfordshire. 322 spp & cvs.*

SCABIOSA
The genus of the scabiouses, but not all of them. Many have been transferred to *Pterocephalus*, *Knautia*, *Cephalaria* and *Succisa. C. caucasica* varieties, the most popular of which is 'Clive Greaves', are the best known.
Woodford, nr Salisbury, Wiltshire.
S. caucasica: *Hardwick Hall, Chesterfield, Derbyshire.*

SCILLA
Spring-flowering bulbs, closely related to Chionodoxa (page 147)
NCCPG London Group, London N5.

SEDUM
Abbey Dore, Hereford & Worcs (See page 99).
Also a collection at Choppington in Northumberland.

SEMPERVIVUM
Hardy, alpine succulents, sometimes called House Leeks.
Bristol, Avon.

SIDALCEA
Hardy herbaceous, easily grown perennials.

Sorbus vilmorinii.
Photo John Kelly.

S. candida is the most widely grown, while 'Rose Queen' is the most popular cultivar.
Colyton, Devon. 28 cvs.

SISYRINCHIUM
Perennials, mostly evergreen, with starry flowers and iris-like foliage.
Newton Abbot, Devon.
Loddon, Norfolk. (See page 127).

SKIMMIA
Evergreen shrubs with fragrant, white flowers and bright red berries.
Royal Botanic Gardens, Kew. 6 spp, 33 cvs
Leicester University Botanic Garden 6 spp, 29 cvs

SLIEVE DONARD
The name of the famous nursery (now no longer extant) at Newcastle, Co. Down, on which many first-class garden plants were raised. This National Collection consists of those plants.
City of Belfast Parks Department.

SORBARIA
Spiraea-like shrubs with pinnate leaves and cloudy plumes of small, white flowers.
Paignton Zoological & Botanical Gardens, Paignton, Devon.

SORBUS
A large genus of trees. Those with pinnate leaves are collectively the Mountain ashes, while those whose leaves are entire are in the group to which the Whitebeam belongs. *Sorbus* are grown for their berries and for their foliage, which is always attractive and often turns to spectacular colour in autumn.
University of Manchester. 40 spp, 32 cvs.
Sections Aria *(Whitebeams etc)* and Micromeles *(botanically different from Aria, but similar)*: *Durham College of Agriculture and Horticulture, Houghall, County Durham.*
The National Trust, Winkworth Arboretum, Godalming, Surrey.

SPIRAEA
Hardy, deciduous flowering shrubs in the rose family, usually with foamy heads of flowers.
Askham Bryan College of Agriculture & Horticulture, York, N Yorkshire.

STERN, SIR FREDERICK
This collection consists of plants selected or raised by Sir Frederick Stern at his home near Worthing, which is open to the public.
Worthing Borough Council, Highdown Gardens, Goring-by-Sea.

STEWARTIA
Camellia-like large shrubs or small trees with beautiful, peeling bark.
Handcross, West Sussex.

STYRACACEAE
The tree and shrub family that includes *Halesia, Styrax, Pterostyrax* and *Sinojackia*. The flowers are usually very snowdrop-like.
Cark-in-Cartmel, Cumbria.

SYMPHYANDRA
A genus of herbaceous perennials related to campanulas.
Padlock Croft, West Wratting, Cambridge. (See page 42).

SYMPHYTUM
Herbaceous perennial plants with fleshy roots. The comfreys.
Broughton, by Biggar, Lanarkshire.

SYRINGA
It is remarkable how this generic name continues to be applied to *Philadelphus*, even though it properly belongs to the lilacs.
Brighton Environmental Services Dept, Withdean Park, London Road, Brighton. 36 spp, 164 cvs
Also a smaller collection in Leeds.

TANACETUM
This collection does not cover the whole of the genus, but just that part which used to be in *Pyrethrum*.
London E4.

TAXUS
The yew genus.
Bedgebury National Pinetum, Bedgebury, Kent.
University of Bath, Claverton Down, Bath.

THALICTRUM
Hardy herbaceous perennials with open sprays of small flowers in summer.
Bridgemere Nurseries, Nantwich, Cheshire. *
Broughton, by Biggar, Lanarkshire.

THYMUS
The thymes, of which there are a great many.
Hexham Herbs, Chollerford, Hexham, Northumberland. *

Right: **Trillium
sessile.**
Photo John Kelly.

Below right:
**Trillium
grandiflorum.**

Kalm Oak Nursery, Ardleigh, Colchester, Essex.*

TILIA
The genus to which lime trees belong.
*Thorpe Perrow Arboretum, Bedale, N. Yorks.
Also a collection in Sussex.*

TILLANDSIA
Air plants. Fascinating bromeliads, most of which require neither water nor soil. They include the 'Spanish Moss' of the southern United States.
nr Wisbech, Cambridgeshire.

TRILLIUM
Hardy herbaceous plants from North America for peaty, shady, moist places. All the flower parts are in threes.
*Chandlers Ford, Hampshire.
Leeds, W. Yorkshire.*

TROLLIUS
Globeflowers.
Ansty, nr Dorchester, Dorset. (See page 103)

TROPAEOLUM
This South American genus includes some of the most sought after climbers and scramblers

of all. It also includes the nasturtiums which are not, however, part of the National Collection.
Broughton, by Biggar, Lanarkshire.

TULBAGHIA
Garlic-scented greenhouse plants. Only two – *T. violacea* and *T.* 'Silver Lace' – are at all widely grown.
Marwood Hill Gardens, Barnstaple, Devon. *

TULIPA

The best collection of historic tulips is at Limmen, Holland. However, one British collection concentrates on old cvs.

Florists' and old tulips: *Shropshire – only 25 cvs.*
Species and primary hybrids: *University Botanic Garden, Cambridge. 63 spp.*

VACCINIUM

Bilberries, blueberries, cranberries and whortleberries.
Greencombe Garden Trust, Porlock, Somerset.

VARIEGATED PLANTS

The National Westminster Bank College, Chipping Norton, Oxfordshire, has 300+ spp and cvs.

VERATRUM

Hardy herbaceous perennials with poisonous rhizomes. A bradycardic (anti-blood pressure) drug is extracted from the root of *Veratrum viride.*
Worplesdon, nr Guildford, Surrey. 9 species.

VERBASCUM

Hardy herbaceous perennials, sub shrubs and alpine shrubs with characteristic "mullein" flowers.

One of several rather similar *Weigela* cultivars.
Photo John Kelly.

University of Birmingham Botanic Gardens.

VERBENA

For a genus of short-lived plants, the number of perennials is remarkable. They bear small, clustered flowers a little like tiny primroses and are scented. The Lemon-Scented Verbena is a shrub belonging to the genus *Aloysia*.
The National Trust for Scotland, Greenbank, Clarkston, Glasgow.

VERONICA SPICATA

This is the only species represented in the National Collection. The cultivars are variations on a low-growing but very variable perennial speedwell, of which 'Crater Lake Blue' is perhaps the best known.
Crondall, Surrey.

VIBURNUM

This large genus of shrubs encompasses species that flower on naked branches in winter, other winter-flowering species (such as the Laurustinus) which are evergreen, several beautiful spring-flowering species, and some that are notable mostly for their foliage (such as *V. rhytidophyllum*). Many are deliciously fragrant.
The National Trust for Scotland, Crathes Castle, Banchory, Kincardineshire.
The Royal Horticultural Society, Hyde Hall Garden, Chelmsford, Essex.
Derby City Council, Friar Gate, Derby.

VINCA

Periwinkle.
Monksilver Nursery, Oakington Road, Cottenham, Cambridge. (See page32).

VIOLA

Violets, violettas and pansies.
***Section* Melanium *(the true pansies)*:**
Swanley, Kent.
Viola odorata: *Cornwall.*
Violas and violettas: *Leeds.*

VITIS VINIFERA

Three National Collections of grape vines have different emphases:-
Principally as fruit: *Brogdale Horticultural Trust, Faversham, Kent.*
Principally for wine-growing in Britain: *Crediton, Devon.**
Principally for grapes under glass: *Reads Nursery, Loddon, Norfolk. (See page 120).* **

WATSONIA

Dramatic, brilliantly coloured bulbs from South Africa, flowering in late summer and needing a mild climate.
East Cowes, Isle of Wight.

WEIGELA

The well known shrubs usually pronounced 'wi-jeel-ia'.
City of Sheffield Botanic Garden, Clarkehouse Road, Sheffield.

WISTERIA

Somerset College of Ag & Hort, Cannington, nr Bridgwater, Somerset. 4 spp, 15 cvs.

YUCCA

American exotics with agave-like leaves and pillars of (usually) white flowers in summer.

Many are hardy.
Somerset Coll of Ag & Hort.

ZANTEDESCHIA

The Arum Lilies, not all of which are white; there is one yellow-flowered species.
nr Canterbury, Kent. 4 species, 32 cultivars (!!)

ZELKOVA

Trees, known as 'Russian Elms'.
Hergest Croft Gardens, Kington, Hereford & Worcs.

ZINGIBERACEAE

The Ginger family. The collection consists of hardy and semi-hardy species and cultivars, such as the Ginger Lilies (*Hedychium* species).
nr Truro, Cornwall.

Above: **A mature, properly pruned wisteria.**
Photo John Kelly.

Left: Zantedeschia aethiopica **'Crowborough'.**
Photo John Kelly.

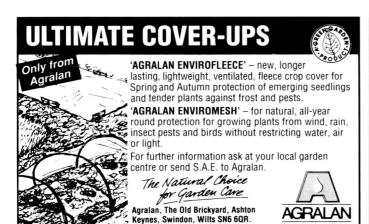

Index

Page numbers in **bold** type relate to captions and illustrations.